Hermeneutics
and the Authority of
Scripture

Task of Theology Today Series
1. *Dogmas and Doctrines,* 1996 edited by Vic Pfitzner and Hilary Regan.
2. *Starting with the Spirit,* 2001 edited by Stephen Pickard and Gordon Preece.
3. *Sin and Salvation,* 2003 edited by Duncan Reid and Mark Worthing.
4. *Theodicy and Eschatology,* 2005 edited by Bruce Barber and David Neville.
5. *Don't Put Out the Burning Bush: Worship and Preaching in a Complex World,* 2008 edited by Vivian Boland OP.

Hermeneutics and the Authority of Scripture

Edited by Alan H Cadwallader

Adelaide
2011

Text copyright © 2011 remains with the individual authors for all papers in this collection.

All rights reserved. Except for any fair dealing permitted under the Copyright Act, no part of this book may be reproduced by any means without prior permission. Inquiries should be made to the publisher.

National Library of Australia Cataloguing-in-Publication entry: (pbk)

Title:	Hermeneutics and the authority of scripture / edited by Alan H Cadwallader.
ISBN:	9781921817151 (pbk.)
Series:	Task of theology today ; 5.
Notes:	Includes index.
Subjects:	Bible--Hermeneutics. Bible--Evidences, authority, etc.
Other Authors/Contributors:	Cadwallader, Alan. Australian Theological Forum.
Dewey Number:	220.6

Cover design by Astrid Sengkey

An imprint of the ATF Ltd
PO Box 504
Hindmarsh, SA 5007
ABN 90 116 359 963
www.atfpress.com

Table of Contents

	Preface	vii
1	Women, Authority and the Bible: Ecological Feminist Considerations *Anne Elvey*	1
2	Interpreting Scripture / Interpreting Law *Frank S Ravitch*	11
3	Hermeneutics and the Authority of Theology: Fusing the Horizons of Hermeneutics and Polanyian Personal Knowledge *Chris Mulherin*	21
4	The Authority of the Bible, the Flood Story, and Problematic Images of God *Terence E Fretheim*	29
5	The Characterisation of God in Lamentations *Elizabeth Boase*	49
6	The Reappropriation of the 'Old' Testament as the Key to Hermeneutical and Ecclesial Renewal *Ockert S Meyer*	65
7	Approaching the New Testament as Source of Faith and Witness to Faith *William Loader*	79

8	Dog-throttling: Nineteenth Century dogmatic / cultural constructions of the Syrophoenician Woman *Alan H Cadwallader*	97
9	Imposing the Silence of Women: A Suggestion about the Date of the Interpolation in 1 Corinthians *Shelly Li*	125
10	Cohesion and Prominence in the Expository Discourse of Colossians *Philip McKeown*	139

List of Contributors 155

Index of Biblical References and Ancient Texts 157

Index of Modern Authors 163

Preface

The question of hermeneutics has increasingly come to dominate all disciplines of human knowledge. It has moved appreciably from a concentration on how to apply the results of research knowledge to considerations of the frameworks by which we conduct research as a meaningful exercise. In this sense contemporary epistemologies and ethical concerns are increasingly seen as critically entwined with the industry of knowledge. The pursuit of meaning has come to be recognised as guiding the very mechanisms that are deployed in the conduct of research. The hermeneutical enterprise therefore is part and parcel of the entry into and the perseverance in research.

Critical analysis of the Bible is no different, even when there is a predisposition or confessional commitment to treat the bible as sacred scripture. Biblical research is inextricably affected by those epistemologies and ethical sensitivities that inform understanding and the search for meaning in our contemporary world.

The essays in this collection amply testify to the breadth of epistemologies and the development of ethical awareness in relation to a range of concerns impacting our world. The reader will find engagements with the Bible informed by developments in science, law, ecology, feminism and linguistics. Key ethical issues about violence, fundamentalism, antisemitism and patriarchy are variously recognised as inextricably involved in the interpretation of the Bible if the Bible is to be handled with responsibility and accountability in today's world. What is clear from these essays is that if the interpreters take hold of the freedom to interpret the Bible in engagement with and critique of structures of knowledge in the contemporary world, then two results follow. Firstly, the Bible re-gains a vibrancy by its re-engagement with human pursuits and, especially, with the human pursuit of knowledge. Indeed, human pursuits and the pursuit of knowledge are themselves invigorated in that re-engagement. Secondly, the Bible is both challenged by and issues a challenge to those very human pursuits, including the pursuit of knowledge. Indeed, as some of these essays argue, the Bible itself demands and reveals in its own fabric such a rigour of hermeneutical engagement.

This collection of essays have been selected primarily from papers that were presented at the *Hermeneutics and the Authority of Scripture* conference held in Canberra in 2007. The Australasian Theological Forum, the organisers of the conference, provided the necessary resources for the keynote speakers at that conference, Terence Fretheim, William Loader and Frances Watson and for the publication of this collection. A number of unforeseen factors stalled the publication of these essays but the resultant collection still speaks powerfully of the radical importance and value of hermeneutics as the guiding dynamism in the continuing authority of the Bible both within confessional communities and in wider cultural interactions. I am grateful to each of the authors in this collection for the wells of patience that they have displayed in awaiting publication. Frances Watson's paper, regrettably, was unable to be included, having already been published elsewhere.

All the essays in this collection, whether drawn from presentations at the conference or received afterwards, were anonymously peer reviewed. I wish to thank those scholars who volunteered their time to select those papers that were suitable for inclusion and who made suggestions for their refinement. Finally, a sincere word of thanks to Hilary Regan and all the support staff at ATF Press who have determinedly pursued a commitment to the publication of fine theological and biblical scholarship in the Australian and New Zealand contexts.

Canberra, 2011 Alan H Cadwallader

Chapter One
Women, Authority and the Bible: Ecological Feminist Considerations

Anne Elvey

When I consider the nexus of women, authority and the Bible from an ecological feminist perspective, I am perplexed. In similar but different ways, feminist, ecojustice and ecocritical approaches to the Bible raise questions about what this text (this book of books) is, why I still engage with it, what it means to me as a member of a Christian community, and how it addresses me in a variety of contexts—as biblical interpreter, as lector, as congregation member, as a woman in a tradition where it remains difficult for women's gifts to be called forth and deepened as 'ordained' for community and world, and, most particularly, as member of a wider, more than human, Earth community.[1]

While the question of women, authority and the Bible is already well-travelled ground, difficulties identified by feminist biblical scholars, such as Elisabeth Schüssler Fiorenza, Letty Russell, Rosemary Radford Ruether, Phyllis Trible, Kwok Pui lan and others over at least twenty-five years have not been addressed adequately in many churches.[2] Meanwhile, feminism

---

1. I use the term 'more than human' coined by David Abram, to describe an Earth community that includes but is much more than the human. For Abram, humans inhabit this 'world' with many Earth others, with whom they are interconnected and toward whom they can be open through human sensuous embodiment. David Abram, *The Spell of the Sensuous* (New York: Vintage Books, 1997).
2. See especially Elisabeth Schüssler Fiorenza's innovative and highly influential book: *In Memory of Her: A Feminist Theological Reconstruction of Christian Origins* (London: SCM, 1983). See also, Kwok Pui-lan, 'Discovering the Bible in the Non-Biblical World', in *Semeia* 47 (1989): 25–42; Rosemary Radford Ruether, 'Feminist Interpretation: A Method of Correlation', in *Feminist Interpretation of the Bible*, edited by Letty M Russell (Oxford: Basil Blackwell, 1985), 111–24; Rosemary Radford Ruether, *Sexism and God-Talk: Toward a Feminist Theology* (London: SCM Press, 1986); Letty M Russell, 'Authority and the Challenge of Feminist Interpretation of the Bible', in *Feminist In-*

itself has changed. Earlier feminisms, founded in a Western liberal democratic framework and appealing to an ideal of equality, have shifted as feminist scholarship has opened itself to a multiplicity of voices, contexts, and approaches.[3]

A prior wave of feminism in the late nineteenth century speaks to this change. Having been active in the abolitionist movement, Elizabeth Cady Stanton became an early advocate for women's suffrage. In her later years, connecting the liberation of women with freedom from biblical gender paradigms, she coordinated and published *The Woman's Bible* in which she described the Bible as the 'words of men' rather than the 'word of God'.[4] While sympathetic to her unease with biblical authority, I want to take from Stanton a different caution: because of her experience of androcentrism within the abolitionist movement and perhaps also her own inherited preference for whiteness, she gave women's liberation higher weight than the emancipation of slaves.[5] Understanding that environmental destruction and oppressions on the basis of race, class or gender are interconnected, can I continue to privilege the category 'woman' or allow 'whiteness' and, in a more than human context, 'humanness', to pass as normative?[6] For those of us who are well fed, sheltered and use more than

---

    terpretation of the Bible, edited by Letty M Russell (Oxford: Basil Blackwell, 1985), 137–46.

3. In feminist biblical studies from the local Australian and Aotearoa New Zealand region, see for example, Judith E McKinlay, *Reframing Her: Biblical Women in Postcolonial Focus* (Sheffield: Sheffield Phoenix Press, 2004); Elaine Wainwright, *Shall We Look for Another? A Feminist Rereading of the Matthean Jesus* (Maryknoll: Orbis Books, 1998); Elaine Wainwright, *Women Healing/Healing Women: The Genderisation of Healing in Early Christianity* (London: Equinox, 2006). Also note the shift signalled in Elisabeth Schüssler Fiorenza's *Discipleship of Equals: A Critical Ekklesia—Logy (Ecclesiology) of Liberation* (London: SCM Press, 1993) which is extended in the multiple approaches of the essays collected in her honour: Fernando F Segovia (editor), *Toward a New Heaven and a New Earth: Essays in Honor of Elisabeth Schüssler Fiorenza* (Maryknoll: Orbis Books, 2003).

4. Elizabeth Cady Stanton (editor), *The Woman's Bible*, 2 vols (Boston: Northeastern University Press, 1993 [1895–1898]) with a foreword by Maureen Fitzgerald, II.8. See also, Lisa S Strange, 'Elizabeth Cady Stanton's *Woman's Bible* and the Roots of Feminist Theology', in *Gender Issues* 17/4 (1999): 15–36.

5. See Jean Fagan Yellin, '"Race" and Nineteenth-Century American Womanhood', in *Legacy* 15/1 (1998): 53–8.

6. On whiteness, see Aileen Moreton-Robinson, *Talkin' up to the White Woman: Indigenous Women and Feminism* (St Lucia: University of Queensland Press, 2000); Suzanne Schech and Jane Haggis, 'Migrancy, Whiteness and the Settler Self in Contemporary Australia', in *Race, Colour and Identity in Australia and New Zealand*, edited by John Docker and Gerhard Fischer (Sydney: UNSW Press, 2000), 231–9.

our share of Earth everyday, perhaps we are past speaking about 'women', authority, and the Bible.

Nevertheless, there is a danger in passing over this topic uncritically. As Barbara Reid writes:

> Any way of telling the story that does not take us more deeply into the freeing and empowering love of God and impel us to radiate that to others is not an adequate version of the story. Nor is it an adequate version if it ignores, trivialises, or increases the sufferings of real women and men, particularly those who suffer most in our world. It is particularly incumbent on preachers, teachers and ministers to tell the story well and to help deconstruct and replace versions that are especially abusive toward women.[7]

Ecofeminist theologians such as Rosemary Radford Ruether, and feminist ecophilosophers such as Val Plumwood, identify a patriarchal—or to take Schüssler Fiorenza's term, 'kyriarchal'—system of hierarchical dualism implicated in oppression of women and destruction of Earth. 'Hierarchical dualism', 'kyriarchy', 'a logic of domination', and 'a logic of colonisation' in practice refer to the same paradigm, where patriarchy is understood as a 'pyramid of multiplicative oppressions', which have feminist, ecological and colonialist effects.[8] For Plumwood, this logic (which is euro-, andro-, and anthropo- centric) is supported by systemic practices of backgrounding (or denial); radical exclusion (or construction as 'other'); incorporation (or assimilation); instrumentalisation; and homogenisation leading to stereotyping and demonisation, particularly in relation to indigenous populations, women, and the wider Earth community construed as 'nature'.[9] In this ecological feminist framework, one might add to Reid's comment, the

---

7. Barbara E Reid, *Taking up the Cross: New Testament Interpretations through Latina and Feminist Eyes* (Minneapolis: Fortress, 2007), 182–3.
8. See Val Plumwood, *Feminism and the Mastery of Nature* (London and New York: Routledge, 1993), 41–68; Rosemary Radford Ruether, *Gaia and God: An Ecofeminist Theology of Earth Healing* (San Francisco: HarperCollins, 1992), 173–201; Elisabeth Schüssler Fiorenza, *But She Said: Feminist Practices of Biblical Interpretation* (Boston: Beacon Press, 1992), 114–20.
9. Plumwood, *Feminism and the Mastery of Nature*, 47–55; Val Plumwood, *Environmental Culture: The Ecological Crisis of Reason* (London: Routledge, 2002), 100–9.

need to be alert to stories that are 'especially abusive in other than human contexts as well as human ones'.

Writing in the first volume of the Earth Bible series, Heather Eaton claims:

> For ecofeminists, the choices are explicit: to accept the patriarchal Bible as sacred and authoritative and be content to expose its patriarchy, or expose its patriarchy and reject it as sacred and authoritative (Milne 1993: 167). From an ecofeminist perspective, the Bible can be accepted only as contingent and provisional (adapted from West 1993:89).[10]

It is difficult to argue with this view, and many feminist readings, uncovering the patriarchal effects of biblical texts, challenge an uncritical acceptance of the authority of the Bible.[11] Among the hermeneutics they employ, a hermeneutics of suspicion emerges that, if seldom sufficient, is always necessary.

Embedding suspicion within a wider hermeneutic circle (or spiral) that moves toward and through creative empowerment, Schüssler Fiorenza recalls:

> On the one hand, the Bible is written in androcentric language, has its origin in the patriarchal cultures of antiquity, and throughout its history has inculcated androcentric and patriarchal values. On the other hand, the Bible has also served to inspire and authorise women and other non-persons in their struggles against patriarchal oppression.[12]

---

10. Heather Eaton, 'Ecofeminist Contributions to an Ecojustice Hermeneutics', in *Readings from the Perspective of Earth*, edited by Norman C Habel, *Earth Bible* (Sheffield: Sheffield Academic Press, 2000), 54–71 at 59. The cross-references are to Patricia Milne, 'The Patriarchal Stamp of Scripture: The Implications of Structural Analyses for Feminist Hermeneutics' in Athalya Brenner (editor), *A Feminist Companion to Genesis* (Sheffield: Sheffield Academic Press, 1993), 146–72 and Cornell West, *Keeping Faith: Philosophy and Race in America* (new York: Routledge, 1993).
11. In recent scholarship, see, for example, Elizabeth V Dowling, *Taking Away the Pound: Women, Theology and the Parable of the Pounds in the Gospel of Luke* (London: T&T Clark, 2007), 214–5.
12. Schüssler Fiorenza, *But She Said*, 21.

Here, Schüssler Fiorenza appeals to two kinds of biblical authority which while in tension may also be interconnected: firstly, a type of normative authority, which as Sandra Schneiders argues can be either 'unilateral and absolute' or 'dialogic and relative' in character, and secondly, an authority to liberate, or authorise those who are oppressed.[13]

From an ecological feminist perspective, I want to suggest a third type of authority that emerges in relation to the embeddedness of the biblical text not only in human community, but also in a wider Earth community: an eco-poetic feminist understanding of biblical authority. Responding to the work of Schüssler Fiorenza, Dorothy Lee writes:

> . . . without denying the importance of political readings, biblical hermeneutics also requires its own poetics, including an understanding of how the text correlates with the modern reader at the narrative, mythic and poetic levels. Here overly-literal notions of how the text impacts on the reader—whether in terms of authorial intention, gender identification or power relations—give way before the unpredictable coalescence between personal experience and poetic/narrative text. Interpretation is ultimately numinous, touching the reader's spiritual and psychological depths.[14]

Lee offers the image of devotion to icons within Eastern Christianity as '[o]ne model that might be helpful in developing a gender-conscious hermeneutical poetics'.[15] Considering 'the ambiguity between image as creative symbol and image as propaganda', she suggests that in a concern to eschew idolatrous patriarchal imagery certain feminist approaches to the Bible have been iconoclastic.[16] Beside this iconoclasm, Lee invites an understanding in which '[s]cripture and icon—sacred myth and sacred image—belong together as 'texts': parallel constructions that unfold a symbolic universe'.[17] A focus for devotion, mediating 'a personal relation-

---

13. Sandra M Schneiders, *The Revelatory Text: Interpreting the New Testament as Sacred Scripture* (Collegeville: Liturgical Press, 2nd edition, 1999), 55–9.
14. Dorothy A Lee, 'Touching the Sacred Text: The Bible as Icon in Feminist Reading', in *Pacifica* 11/3 (1998): 249–64 at 250.
15. *Ibid*, 251.
16. *Ibid*, 255–9.
17. *Ibid*, 256.

ship between the viewer and the divine realm', the icon becomes for Lee a metaphor for the Bible.[18]

Lee identifies four points of similarity between the Bible and the icon:
1. the icon is not identical to the sacred reality it portrays or conveys;
2. the sense of presence the icon communicates exceeds rational deliberation on its meaning or construction;
3. the icon is non-dualistic but represents a union of matter and spirit, divine and human, body and soul;
4. there is a mutuality between subject and subject: the icon as subject of devotion or contemplation and the viewer as subject under the gaze of the icon.[19]

To open up an eco-poetic feminist reflection on authority and the Bible, I will focus very briefly on two aspects of the icon:
1. the relationship between the icon and the matter from which it is formed; and
2. the effect of the icon on the subjectivity of the viewer.

Concerning the world of the icon, John Chryssavgis writes that in the icon 'there is no sharp line of demarcation between "material" and "spiritual". The icon constitutes the epiphany of God in the world and the existence of the world in the presence of God.'[20] Recently, in a time of transition, I undertook a short course on icon painting, where we learnt that the painting of an icon is a movement from darkness to light. The darker undercolours of flesh, garments, hair, and background are painted in on the smoothed gesso surface *first*. Then the first layer of light and shadow is added. Finally, the highlights and gold leaf are applied. The paints are mixed from natural pigments: ochres and semi precious metals. The light in the icon emerges from the application of these material elements, these bits of Earth. In part at least, it is this inner light of matter (rather than a reflected light) that engages the viewer in a dynamic interplay between the

---

18. *Ibid*, 251.
19. *Ibid*, 256–61.
20. John Chryssavgis, 'The World of the Icon and Creation: An Orthodox Perspective on Ecology and Pneumatology', in *Christianity and Ecology: Seeking the Well-Being of Earth and Humans*, edited by Dieter T Hessel and Rosemary Radford Ruether (Cambridge, Mass: Harvard University Press, 2000), 83–96 at 84. See also, Gerald L Sittser, 'Protestant Missionary Biography as Written Icon', in the *Christian Scholar's Review* 36/3 (2007): 303–21.

prototype (the one represented in the icon), the particular icon itself and the person revering it.[21]

With the Bible we are dealing less directly with material elements, but they are there. Papyrus, parchment, paper, ink, even the light and shade on a computer screen when we read the text from a CD-rom or from an internet site, are grounded in matter: papyrus plants, animal skins, trees, minerals, fossils.[22] The writers of the text themselves were nourished by and within an Earth community; the language emerged in human bodies and interrelationships, in the embodied breath and mind.[23] So, the text is not a creation *ex nihilo*, but a materially grounded thing. From this perspective, biblical authority—subtended by matter, where matter is taken in the widest sense as all that makes up the organic and inorganic physicality of Earth and cosmos[24]—is relational and incarnational. While Chryssavgis writes that '[t]he icon presupposes and even proposes another means of communication, beyond the conceptual, written, or spoken word', I want to affirm that, in their communication through the human mediation of matter, both icon and Bible, are 'sacramental'.[25]

In this respect, Chryssavgis describes the icon as 'transfigurative' rather than 'figurative' or 'nonfigurative'.[26] The biblical paradigm for iconography (icon writing), then, is the story of the transfiguration (Matt 17:1-9, Mk 9:2-10, Lk 9:28-36). In different ways, each of the synoptic accounts has the disciples unsettled by the encounter in which Jesus is revealed as the icon of God dwelling within the materiality of the cosmos.[27] With Jesus' passion and death in view (especially Lk 9:31), the transfiguration accounts call forth the divine image restored in a humanity embedded

---

21. Anna Kartsonis, 'The Responding Icon', in *Heaven on Earth: Art and the Church in Byzantium*, edited by Linda Safran (University Park, Penn: The Pennsylvania State University Press, 1998), 58-80 at 60.
22. Anne F Elvey, *An Ecological Feminist Reading of the Gospel of Luke: A Gestational Paradigm* (Lewiston: Edwin Mellen Press, 2005), 25.
23. Compare Abram, *The Spell of the Sensuous*, 73-92.
24. This view parallels Catherine Keller's perspective on creation, when she re-reads Genesis 1:2 against a tradition of creation *ex nihilo*, to affirm an unsettling interagency between creator and the stuff/matter of creation. See Catherine Keller, *Face of the Deep: A Theology of Becoming* (London: Routledge, 2003) especially at 238.
25. Chryssavgis, 'The World of the Icon', 87.
26. *Ibid.*
27. John Gatta, 'The Transfiguration of Christ and Cosmos: A Focal Point of Literary Imagination', in the *Sewanee Theological Review* 49/4 (2006): 484-506 especially at 490, 498.

within a more than human Earth community (compare Gen 1:26-28).[28] Even if the disciples do not in the narrative context immediately experience a lasting shift of worldview on the mountain, the accounts stand as windows into and calls to such a shift. For Chryssavgis, the icon can occasion in the viewer a similar shift of worldview or perspective.[29]

For Julia Kristeva, the Bible, too, has the capacity to unsettle our subjectivities.[30] In reading the Bible, one is engaged with an otherness both inscribed in, and exceeding, not only the text but also the patriarchal imaginaries of authority brought into play in association with it and with certain influential traditions of biblical reception and interpretation.[31] This shifting or unsettling of worldview is not (or need not be) simply a momentary discomfort, but rather opens the possibility for transformation that, like the biblical transfiguration accounts, does not turn away from the death of that worldview, a turning that would threaten to close off possibility.

Referring to Adrienne Rich's poem 'Power', Schüssler Fiorenza describes 'women's biblical heritage as one and the same source for women's religious power and suffering'.[32] In addressing the biblical text in our contemporary situation of ecological trauma, can we turn this around to say that *our power/authority comes from the same source as our wounds*—with '*our*' read broadly as referring to our being constituted within a more than human Earth community, and the biblical heritage understood to be but one source of our wounding, both that wounding we suffer and that which we occasion? Then the encounter between text and reader can offer the possibility of transformation oriented toward healing: personal, social and cultural.

Through openness to the otherness of text and context, this transformative encounter receives structure through the discipline of critical reading practices. In her recent work on women and healing in the synoptic gospels, Elaine Wainwright, for example, develops a transformative hermeneutics using feminist, postcolonial and ecological lenses along with the tools of socio-rhetorical criticism, in a process of theological meaning-

---

28. *Ibid.*
29. Chryssavgis, 'The World of the Icon', 83-4.
30. Julia Kristeva, 'Reading the Bible', in *New Maladies of the Soul* (New York: Columbia University Press, 1995), 115-26.
31. *Ibid.*
32. Schüssler Fiorenza, *But She Said*, 21; see Adrienne Rich, *The Dream of a Common Language* (New York: Norton, 1993), 3.

making that is itself directed toward healing.[33] Affirming this orientation toward transformation, can we consider an authority *in* (rather than *of*) the biblical text, where the text is a place of vibrant interrelationship between material elements, human languages, writers and readers? In this dynamic mediated materiality, an inner light or voice can emerge in our contemplative critical engagement with the text, when we are both open and opened to a multitude of others: human and other than human, past, present and future, especially as we think of ourselves as ancestors of those who will inhabit Earth after us.

---

33. Wainwright, *Women Healing/Healing Women*.

Chapter Two
Interpreting Scripture / Interpreting Law

Frank S Ravitch

Introduction

Scholars have frequently noted the similarities between interpreting scripture and interpreting law, especially interpreting a Constitution. There are, of course, significant differences as well. The field of 'Biblical' hermeneutics—theories of interpretation—has a long history, as does the field of legal hermeneutics. Moreover, much has been written on the relationship between religious interpretation and legal interpretation.[1]

This essay is not meant to provide even a basic overview of these rich and diverse fields of inquiry. Rather, the focus is on some of the vexing problems facing those who utilise what this essay refers to as 'dogmatic' approaches to interpreting religion or law. The focus here will be on biblical interpretation and constitutional interpretation. Specifically, I will compare biblical literalism with textualism and originalism. As will be seen these approaches suffer from problems of translation both figuratively and literally (in the case of Biblical literalism in the US).

---

1. Some examples of excellent articles addressing this include, Thomas C Grey, 'The Constitution as Scripture', in the *Stanford Law Review* 37 (1984): 1-25; Howard Lesnick, 'The Consciousness of Religion and the Consciousness of Law, With Some Implications for Dialogue', in the *University of Pennsylvania Journal of Constitutional Law* 8 (2006): 335–54; Michael J Perry, 'The Authority of Text, Tradition, and Reason: A Theory of Constitutional "Interpretation"', in the *Southern California Law Review* 58 (1985): 551–80; Maimon Schwarzschild, 'Pluralist Interpretation: From Religion to the First Amendment', in the *Journal of Contemporary Legal Issues* 7 (1996): 447–72; see also Sanford Levinson, *Constitutional Faith* (Princeton: Princeton University Press, 1988) (comparing religious and constitutional interpretation in the context of a broader discussion 'civil religion').

Drifting Unreflectively through Language and Time: The Joys of Dogmatism

Biblical literalism is highly problematic unless one reads ancient Hebrew (old testament), Greek and/or Aramaic (new testament). Claiming to take the words of the bible literally without being fluent in these languages is like claiming to take every word of a work of complex Greek philosophy literally without understanding Greek. Translations are not perfect even when translators use their best efforts. Some translations, such as the King James bible, are even more problematic because they also served a political function.[2]

Even if one could literally translate from one language into another without losing, changing, or augmenting meaning, the problems of cultural and historical shifts remain.[3] When one claims to take the words of the bible literally one not only ignores the problem of translation from language to language, but also the problem of *dasein* (being in the world). We are the products of our traditions and cultural embeddedness.[4] When we try to understand historical texts we tend to bring them forward to our time and/or attempt to put ourselves back in the period when they were written. Yet, we did not live in that time or culture and it is hard to escape our horizon (view of the world) when we engage with the text. Therefore, we may fail to consider accurately what the words meant in the culture and time when they were written.[5]

Of course, many theologians have long recognised this and many faiths are not literalist in the sense of taking every word of holy texts to be literally true without the need for interpretation.[6] These theologians understand that even literalists are interpreting. Literalists sometimes don't realise or acknowledge that they are doing so, but they cannot escape interpreting holy texts (or interpreting generally).[7] One way to address this is the recognition by some Protestant theologians that if one is sufficiently

---

2. Benson Bobrick, *Wide as the Waters: The Story of the English Bible and the Revolution it Inspired* (Harmondsworth, England: Penguin, 2002).
3. See below.
4. Hans-Georg Gadamer, *Truth and Method* translated by Joel Weinsheimer and Donald G Marshall (London / New York: Continuum, 2nd revised edition, 1999), 257–64.
5. Frank S Ravitch, *Masters of Illusion: The Supreme Court and the Religion Clauses* (New York: New York University Press, 2007), 2–6, 9–11, 81–82
6. In fact, the number of faiths and denominations that acknowledge interpretation occurs in understanding and applying religious texts far outnumber those which do not.
7. See Gadamer, above.

connected to Jesus one can understand the teaching in the bible despite these linguistic, cultural and historical voids.[8] The problem here is that many who claim to be sufficiently connected to Jesus and to interpret the text literally disagree with each other as to its meaning. There is no Archimedean point from which we can say, from outside a given tradition, that person X has the real Jesus in her heart and therefore her understanding is the correct one.[9]

Many religions and religious individuals understand this and eschew biblical literalism in favor of more complex biblical hermeneutics (theories of interpretation). These religions generally take holy texts quite seriously, but they understand that interpretation is part of understanding any text. Moreover, some of these faiths are especially wary of human claims to take the words of holy texts literally, given that these texts are generally considered to have been authored by, or inspired by, the divine. This raises obvious problems with assuming, or even understanding, what we might call the intent of the framer. These faiths take the task of interpretation seriously, and methodically try to understand holy texts.[10]16 Whether they are correct in their interpretations is irrelevant to the present discussion. The key is that they understand that texts often need to be interpreted and that to do so one may need linguistic skills and an awareness of the problems of translating across time and cultures.[11]

Interestingly, in the realm of constitutional interpretation strict textualists and hard originalists have a lot in common with biblical literalists. A number of scholars and judges have noted the problems inherent in strict textualism. Except in the easiest cases—cases where the constitutional text is not subject to more than one interpretation *and* where the text can be easily applied to the facts of the case in dispute—strict textualism is impossible. Some would say it is impossible even then, but I am unwilling to go that far. Of course there are few such cases, and many judges and scholars would agree that in these cases looking only to the text is the best approach. In the bulk of cases this approach is unavailable because either

---

8. Grey, 'Constitution as Scripture', 5–6.
9. Compare Gadamer, above, implying one must already be influenced by, or be part of, the tradition in order to reach meaning based on that tradition. Those outside the tradition may have very different preconceptions, and Ravitch, above, addressing the problems with accepting any universal principle or concept without interpretation and the effect of preconceptions in that interpretation.
10. See Grey, 'Constitution', 5–9.
11. See below

the constitutional text is not clear and/or because the text can not be mechanically applied to the case at hand.

As a result many judges and scholars look to the intent of the framers to help interpret the Constitution. The notion is that the intent of the framers helps an interpreter to understand the text and that it provides an objective restraint on judicial interpretation.[12] As I have argued elsewhere, at least in highly contested interpretive scenarios, neither of these assumptions are accurate. In fact, at least as to the latter assumption about objectivity, quite the opposite might be true; reliance on original intent may simply mask judicial predispositions because the intent of the framers may be unknowable or divided.[13] Moreover, as H Jefferson Powell has suggested it is possible that the intent of the framers was not to follow the strict intent of the framers.[14]

This is particularly interesting in the context of biblical literalism. If G-d is the author of the bible, either directly or through inspiration, how does one know his intent? In fact, how does one know whether the text was intended as metaphor, simply to teach lessons, or to be literally read. Is G-d's intent not to expect humans to guess at his intent, but rather to use our G-d given capacities to apply biblical teachings to everyday life? How can this be done without interpretation? These are ancient theological questions that certainly can not be answered in this brief essay. They demonstrate, however, the hubris that seems to drive much dogmatic literalist interpretation, whether biblical or constitutional. Biblical literalists believe they know what the biblical text means even if they do not speak or understand the languages it was written in, and even if based on the text alone there are alternative interpretations.[15] Strict constitutional textualists and hard originalists share similar beliefs. They too often believe their interpretation of the text is the correct one, even where other textual interpretations exist. Hard originalists believe that they can know the intent of the framers even where that intent is not clear, may have varied among the framers, or may have varied even within the hearts and minds of individual framers. Moreover, the modern interpreters did not live in

---

12. See Steven G Calabresi (editor), *Originalism: a Quarter-Century of Debate* (Washington: Regnery Publications, 2007).
13. Ravitch, *Masters of Illusion*, 2–6, 81–2.
14. H Jefferson Powell, 'The Original Understanding of Original Intent' in the *Harvard Law Review* 98 (1985): 885–948.
15. John Bartkowski, 'Beyond Biblical Literalism and Inerrancy: Conservative Protestants and the Hermeneutic Interpretation of Scripture' in *Sociology of Religion* 57 (1996): 259–72.

the time of the framers and may have significantly different preconceptions.[16]

In the end interpretation is inescapable. Perhaps this is the biggest stumbling block for those who wish to engage in dogmatic textual exegesis. Many eschew interpretation and hold tightly to notions of objectivity and clarity, yet the best they can hope for in this regard is the production of an illusion of clarity and objectivity. Underneath this illusion the same interpretive questions, and the attendant metaphysical questions, remain.

Taking the Hermeneutic Turn

It seems interpretation is necessary to apply core texts to real world situations, whether those core texts be religious or a nation's core text such as a constitution. Hermeneutics are an inescapable part of everyday life. We are always interpreting, whether we know it or not. This is even more true when one attempts to apply a text written in a different time and culture to situations arising today. There are many approaches to interpretation, and many of these overlap on salient points. As I have written elsewhere, however, philosophical hermeneutics seems especially useful in the context of constitutional interpretation because of the time lag and cultural shifts between the drafting of the constitution and the present.[17] For similar reasons, this approach — which was clearly influenced in part by biblical hermeneutics[18]—is helpful in analysing the interpretation of religious texts.

The philosopher Hans-Georg Gadamer explained that there is no absolute method of interpretation.[19] Each interpreter brings his or her own preconceptions into the act of interpreting a text.[20] These preconceptions are influenced by the tradition, including social context, in which the interpreter exists.[21] The interpreter's tradition(s) provides her with a horizon that includes her interpretive predispositions. This horizon is the range of

---

16. Ravitch, *Masters of Illusion*, 2–6, 9–11, 81–2.
17. Ravitch, *Masters of Illusion*, 9–11.
18. Jean Grondin, *Introduction to Philosophical Hermeneutics* translated by Joel Weinsheimer (New Haven: Yale University Press, 1994).
19. This is a primary point in his *Truth and Method*. See also his *Reason in the Age of Science* translated by Frederick G Lawrence (Cambridge, Mass: MIT Press, 1981).
20. Gadamer, *Truth and Method*, 265–71. Text can refer to more than just a written text.
21. See William N Eskridge, Jr, 'Gadamer / Statutory Interpretation', in *Columbia Law Review* 90 (1990): 621–22.

what the interpreter can see when engaging with a text.[22] The concept of *dasein*, or being in the world, captures this dynamic. We exist in the world around us and that world influences how we view things.[23] Thus, our traditions and context are a part of our being. The anthropologist Clifford Geertz observed this while studying other cultures.[24]

Still, the text has its own horizon of meaning.[25] That horizon is influenced by the context (or tradition) in which it was written, those influencing or interpreting it over the passage of time, the words used, and the context of the original author or authors.[26] Philosophical hermeneutics suggests that to understand a text a give and take must occur between text and interpreter, a dialogue between one's being and the object that one seeks to understand.[27] This conversation transforms both the text and interpreter as they engage in the give and take.[28]

The interpreter necessarily projects his or her horizon into the interpretive process, but should also reflect upon it and the horizon of the text.[29] The horizon of the text has a binding quality in that if the interpreter openly enters into dialogue with the text, the horizon of the text will limit the range of preconceptions the interpreter can project consistently with the horizon of the text.[30] Since the text and interpreter are engaged in a dialogue to reach a common truth, neither text nor interpreter are the sole source of meaning.

Gadamer saw the quest for interpretive methodologies as interfering with the process of interpretation by obfuscating what is really going on. It is not that interpretive methodology is useless, but rather that it does not do what it purports to do—reach an objective and unquestionable meaning. The process of reaching meaning requires a constant dialogue between text and interpreter. This dialogue is mediated, however, by tradition (I prefer the term 'context').[31]

---

22. Gadamer, *Truth and Method*, 302–7, 374–75.
23. Gadamer, *Truth and Method*, 257–64.
24. Clifford Geertz, *The Interpretation of Cultures* (New York: Basic Books, 1973).
25. Gadamer, *Truth and Method*, 302–7.
26. Gadamer, *Truth and Method*, 370, 374–5; *Reason in the Age of Science*, 98. This may actually be an under inclusive list.
27. This dialogue is central to Gadamer's theory of interpretation.
28. Gadamer, *Truth and Method*, 307.
29. Gadamer, *Truth and Method*, 267–9.
30. Eskridge, 'Gadamer / Statutory Interpretation', 627.
31. Gadamer, *Truth and Method*, 266–7, 276–7.

Significantly, Gadamer does not believe that the lack of a clear interpretive method prevents one from reaching truth (understanding). It simply demonstrates that truth can be variable when different texts and interpreters engage in the hermeneutic dialogue, or when that dialogue is engaged in over time by the same interpreter. This is not a form of relativism as some critics have suggested.[32] Through a dialogue between text and interpreter one can reach a better understanding of the text than one who does not engage in such dialogue and simply assigns a reflexive meaning to the text. Thus, while there is no methodological approach to interpretation in Gadamerian hermeneutics, there is a way for text and interpreter to interact to reach a meaning that is both consistent with the text and cognizant of the role the interpreter plays in reaching that meaning.

Concluding Thoughts: The Failure of Dogmatic Methodologies in Constitutional and Scriptural Interpretation

If we are embedded creatures—embedded in our traditions and context—as the concept of *dasein* suggests, there is no Archimedean point from which we can say that a given methodology is objective, at least in contested interpretive contexts. This does not mean nihilism must reign. After all, as Gadamer points out the dialogue between text and interpreter can lead to meaning, and because the interpreter must throw out preconceptions that are inconsistent with the horizon of the text in order to fuse horizons and interpret, it seems obvious that the interpretive possibilities are limited to the range of what fits within both the horizon of the interpreter and the horizon of the text. Legal interpreters generally use a variety of interpretive modes from within the legal tradition when interpreting the Constitution.[33] The key question is whether claims that these modes provide objective methods of interpretation are anything more than illusion. Similar questions arise in the context of scriptural interpretation, but there the possible modes of interpretation may vary significantly between, and even within, faiths.

This essay is focused strictly on what I refer to as dogmatic modes of interpretation. Thus, it is not meant as a detailed discussion of constitutional or scriptural hermeneutics. For present purposes the only question is whether biblical literalism and the combination of strict constitutional

---

32. Grondin, *Philosophical Hermeneutics*, 141–2.
33. See Philip Bobbit, *Constitutional Fate* (Oxford: Oxford University Press, 1984), *Constitutional Interpretation* (Oxford: Blackwell, 1991), Ravitch, *Masters of Illusion*, 6–8.

textualism and originalism have anything in common and anything useful to offer interpreters? As noted above, they do have quite a bit in common; although there are also significant differences. As for the second question the answer depends on whether one finds the solace folks might derive from a false sense of objectivity to be useful to interpreters. Both biblical literalism and strict textualism / originalism fail to address the problem of determining intent, in the first case from the divine (either directly or through inspiration) and, in the second, from a diverse group of framers and ratifiers. Moreover, these approaches fail to account for the influence of time, culture, and tradition on the meaning of a text that must be applied in a different time, culture and at least partially different tradition.

The answer seems obvious. Strict biblical literalism—in the sense that one can derive *the* meaning of biblical text from the text without any interpretation, and usually a translated text at that, is impossible. Interpretation happens whether acknowledged or not and human preconceptions necessarily enter the fray. Of course, one may take on faith that such literal interpretation is possible either because one is sufficiently imbued with the spirit of G-d to know what the text means or one simply has faith that *the* interpretation is correct.[34] Such beliefs do not change the interpretive reality, however, that unless one shares that faith the intervention of human preconceptions and traditions in the interpretive process cannot be ignored.

Constitutional interpreters can not fall back on such faith arguments, however. The job of interpreting a constitution and applying it to current cases and issues is part of the legal and legislative traditions, and these traditions create a need for justifications beyond the assertion, 'I have faith I can channel the spirit of the framers'. When the text is reasonably clear and its application seems obvious the traditions of legal interpretation will generally point toward a specific answer or smaller range of answers as the interpreter engages with the text. These are commonly called the 'easy cases'. Often, however, the text or its application is not so clear. I like to call these, a bit tongue in cheek, 'most cases'. In such cases, strict textualism simply does not have the tools to answer the question. Simply put, it cannot do what it sets out to accomplish, provide objective answers to questions without relying on judicial preconceptions. As I have written elsewhere, originalism suffers the same flaw.[35] In fact, originalism is doubly problematic. Unless there is a clear, overarching, and uncontested

---

34. Grey, 'Constitution as Scripture', 5–6.
35. Ravitch, *Masters of Illusion*, 2–6.

sense of the framers and ratifiers, an interpreter must be using preconceptions to choose which intent he or she applies to a given interpretive situation. Even when there does seem to be clear, overarching and uncontested agreement among the framers and ratifiers one must be careful in applying that intent to the modern context given the different culture, time and traditions in which that intent existed, and the need to interpret in order to bring that intent forward to the current case or situation.[36]

Like biblical literalists, strict textualists and originalists seem to have a deep faith in the objectivity of their approaches. The ultimate question is whether this faith is grounded in greater objectivity given that greater objectivity and reigning in the application of judicial preconceptions seem to be the bases for relying on strict textualism and originalism. This brief essay asserts that the answer is a guarded no.

---

36. Ravitch, *Masters of Illusion*, 2–6, 9–11, 81–2.

Chapter Three
Hermeneutics and the Authority of Theology: Fusing the Horizons of Hermeneutics and Polanyian Personal Knowledge

Chris Mulherin

The apologetic issue the Church faces as it commends its truth claims to a secular world is not so much that of biblical authority as that of theological authority. In what sense can a secular world dominated by science take theological knowledge claims seriously? After all, science is about knowledge, truth and reality, while theology is about faith, belief and what can at best be described as subjective truth. Or perhaps not.

This essay outlines the epistemology of Michael Polanyi and highlights how his work complements hermeneutical theory. Polanyi turned to philosophy from a distinguished career as a scientist, publishing over two hundred papers. For him, objective knowledge, understood as knowledge that is impersonally detached and foolproof, is a contradiction in terms. As human agents we are inescapably committed to acting in faith upon sincere beliefs that we hold to be universally true. This we can do with confidence only when we have seen the error of equating knowledge with impersonal objectivism.

In this paper I outline Polanyi's view of knowledge and reality and then suggest that Polanyi's 'personal knowledge' bridges the gap between faith and science, and between hermeneutic understanding and scientific explanation. While science and theology study different aspects of reality they do so in remarkably similar ways, both resulting in 'personal knowledge'.

My project involves a bringing together of theological and philosophical hermeneutics with Michael Polanyi's view of scientific knowledge. This work arises out of research I did on Polanyi years ago and an intuition—also shared by many of his fans—that Polanyi's explanation of the scientific pursuit is remarkably amenable to theological adaptation. More specifically, I want to flesh out some theological aspects of what one scholar has called 'the striking resemblance between Polanyi's model of scientific understanding... and Gadamer's model of hermeneutical understanding' both of which are based on a critique of objectivism within their fields of interest.[1]

But here I hope simply to give us a taste of Polanyi's view of the natural sciences and indicate how such a view opens an apologetic door for theological realism. Why apologetic? My thinking is this: the common view of science—that it guarantees impersonal and objective truth about reality—has contributed to skepticism about all things non-scientific. On these grounds the possibility of theological truth claims seems ludicrous to many and in this sense the authority of theology in the marketplace of ideas is gravely in question. My suggestion is that such skepticism would be chastened if the true nature of the scientific endeavor were better understood.

Let me set the stage by citing one of my students from years past. He said:

> I believe there are no correct answers to moral questions,
> ... only what individuals believe to be correct.... It can quite
> clearly be seen from [the abortion] question that there is no
> right or wrong answer, only what the individual believes to
> be right or wrong. The question is quite clearly a matter of
> taste where there can be a variety of answers. It cannot be
> scientifically proven whether women should be permitted to
> terminate pregnancies.

In a nutshell, this quotation captures the problem we are wrestling with today. The problem implicitly raised by my student might be put like this: how can we take the possibility of moral knowledge and by corollary theological knowledge seriously in an enlightened scientific world; a world where we know that true, objective and impersonal knowledge comes from science; a world where we know that religion and morality are relative, personal, subjective and merely a matter of taste?

The reason for using this quotation is not to provoke moral debate. The point is that my student's argument rests on a commonly held view of

---

1. Robert Innis, 'In Memoriam Michael Polanyi', in *Zeitschrift für allgemeine Wissenschaftstheorie* 8/1 (1977): 22-9.

science as the epitome of truth, and the only means of access to non-subjective reality. Central to this modern mythology is the belief that there is a yawning chasm between two sorts of human pursuits: We have the mutual exclusivity of knowledge and belief, of objectivity and subjectivity. We have facts and values, we have truth and opinion, we have proof and ignorance and we have certainty and faith, each one polar opposites. We call one side the realm of science and the other we call religion or philosophy or, in the ultimate of put-downs, we simply call the other side 'non-science'. The inevitable result is that it goes without saying that reality lies on one side of the chasm while theology as well as morality and aesthetics lie on the other.

It is this view of knowledge and reality that is implicitly summed up by my student when he says that there are no correct answers because there is no scientific proof. While my student may have been ignorant of the fact, there are clear echoes of Nietzsche's dictum that, ' . . . there are no moral facts whatever. Moral judgment has this in common with religious judgment, that it believes realities which do not exist.'[2]

Let's turn now to Michael Polanyi's view of science. In his *magnum opus* called *Personal Knowledge* Polanyi, already a successful world-class scientist, expressed his objective as follows, 'The principal purpose of this book is to achieve a frame of mind in which I may hold firmly to what I believe to be true, even though I know that it might conceivably be false.'[3]

In an intellectual climate where knowledge is equated with objectivism and certainty, it seems grossly insufficient to talk of holding to what we believe to be true, even if we know it might be false. Polanyi's 'personal knowledge' not only challenges those views that accept the possibility of detached, objective knowledge but it also undermines those views which, while they reject the *practical* possibility of objectivity, nevertheless accept the *ideal* of knowledge as objective and impersonal. In this sense, Polanyi rewrites the rules about what counts as 'knowledge' by showing the incoherence of the way the concept is commonly used.

Polanyi shows that 'objective knowledge', understood as impersonal, detached and foolproof, is a contradiction in terms and that as human beings we are inescapably committed to acting in faith upon sincere beliefs which we hold to be universally true. This we can do with confidence only when we have seen the error of equating knowledge with impersonal ob-

---

2. F Nietzsche, *Twilight of the Idols*, translated by RJ Hollingdale (Harmondsworth, UK: Penguin, 1968), 55.
3. M Polanyi, *Personal Knowledge* (London: Routledge and Kegan Paul, 1958), 214.

jectivism. But this must not be seen as a retreat into subjectivism for while we may not claim sure knowledge, we may still claim that our beliefs are about the real world and that they are universally true.

The contrast and challenge to common understandings of science that this view presents is clear, for the explicit aim of science is to establish an impersonal and objective knowledge. And in so far as science falls short of this ideal it is seen as a temporary state to be rectified by more and better science. But Polanyi's suggestion that there is an indispensable tacit element in all human knowing means that the ideal of attempting to eliminate all personal elements of knowledge would, in effect, be aiming at the destruction of all knowledge.[4]

One approach to justifying the validity and reality of religious truth is to argue with Nietzsche's position by trying to show somehow or other the possibility of objective theological knowledge. An example might be an apologetic that claims to argue scientifically for the existence of God or more polemically, for a young earth creation on biblical grounds. But this approach, which doesn't question the objectivist view of knowledge, suffers from the same self-defeating misunderstanding about the nature of scientific beliefs that Polanyi exposed: it consists in accepting the received view of science and arguing that theology can be done the same way.

Another response of the theological fraternity is firstly to accept implicitly the received view of science as the only source of universal truth about any extra-human reality, and then to agree that theology does not meet such criteria. And so while theology might be appealing and personally significant it is ruled out of making universal truth claims.

My suggested starting point though is not to accept the view that theology can't make claims about the things of God as science does about the natural world. Nor is the way forward to dress up theology in the scientific emperor's clothes in order to make it look more credible by conforming to an incoherent view of ideal knowledge.

To put it in simple terms, it's not that theology has to be like science to be credible. It's that we need to trumpet to the sceptic that science in practice is already like theology. That is, they are both hermeneutic exercises where the outcome is personal knowledge held to be true with universal intent. Personal because it is the result of a fiduciary act of commitment and universal because its claimed object is not just 'true for me' but is grounded in reality independent of the knower.

---

4. See M Polanyi, *The Tacit Dimension* (London: Routledge and Kegan Paul, 1967), 20.

Let me turn to Polanyi's epistemology. Polanyi would say that in order to demonstrate the incoherence of the 'detached objectivity' view of knowledge it is sufficient to show that all knowledge must necessarily involve a personal, non-objective, element that in the last analysis is unspecifiable. This tacit component of knowledge involves a personal commitment on the part of the knower that is based ultimately and inevitably on faith. To know anything, such commitments are always involved; a step of faith, for which no certain or further justification can be offered. Hence all knowledge is personal knowledge; something believed without ultimate proof by a knowing subject to be true.

One of Polanyi's key insights is summed up in his phrase, 'we know more than we can tell.'[5] Polanyi showed that in all scientific knowledge and especially in the process of discovery there is always and inevitably a tacit coefficient, a hidden element, which is an essential aspect of our knowledge but which we do not focus upon. And in fact it is often impossible to focus upon this aspect explicitly. We know more than we can tell.

Is it possible, for example, to explain exactly how to ride a bike? Those who know how to ride a bicycle also know that we know, although as we ponder it we recognise that we cannot tell precisely what it is to know how to ride. That is, we know something that we cannot tell. And if someone happens to tell us the mathematical formula governing bike riding we are still likely to maintain that we knew how to ride a bike without being able to formalise it explicitly. And for those who would like to learn to ride, the essence is this: when you are off balance you need to perform the counter intuitive action of turning into the direction of fall so that the radius of curvature is proportional to the square of your linear velocity and inversely proportional to the tangent of the angle of lean. Simple really!

Or take another example: how would someone define precisely how to go about recognising the face of one's mother or child in a crowd? What are the explicit characteristics of that familiar face that one could describe to others so that they too would infallibly recognise them if they met them? If a person has trouble with an exact definition does this mean that she really doesn't know what her mother looks like? Such a suggestion would bring the rebuttal that in fact the person does know that face even if she can't specify explicitly how she knows.

To give similar examples from science, think of how much time is spent by the budding geologist in learning the art of recognising rock

---

5. Polanyi, *Personal Knowledge*, x; *Tacit Dimension*, 8.

specimens, or the biology or botany student coming to grips with classification systems that in the last analysis are unspecifiable. Or what about an explicit biological definition of what a human being is? It proves impossible to come up with a definition that includes every example of the species and eliminates every being that is not human. And here you may recognise a problem that is fundamental to the issue at hand; we beg our own question when we assume that which we are setting out to define. With respect to defining what a human being is: we cannot even begin to look for common characteristics of human beings unless we are already confident we know which specimens to examine in the first place.

It is this circular, or perhaps hermeneutic, logic that is crucial to what I am suggesting and we need to recognise that all human beliefs, including scientific claims to knowledge, also beg the question in the same way. The biologist does not define life but rather tries to identify in an organised manner that which is already known and recognised. The doctor who recognises a new disease cannot do so by rules that unfailingly identify that disease, for as yet it doesn't even have a name let alone a reference in a medical textbook. Nevertheless, this lack of explicit rules and identifying symptoms does not prevent us believing that new diseases do exist in reality and are identified.

What Polanyi convincingly shows us is the fact that this sort of highly personal, tacit knowledge, which is neither formal nor explicit, is necessary for science and indeed any human activity to proceed. In the words of one commentator on Polanyi's work:

> There is no purely objective knowledge, because nothing can be called knowledge that is not personally accredited as knowledge. Facts do not force themselves upon us. What we call 'facts' always involve our judgment (with some degree of risk) that something *is* a fact. What is acknowledged as a fact is, of course, something in which we must believe. But it is so acknowledged because we first do, in fact, believe it . . . In a different way subjective knowledge would also be a contradiction in terms. The purely subjective has reference only to the person involved.[6]

---

6. Harry Prosch, *Michael Polanyi: A Critical Exposition* (Albany: State University of New York Press, 1986), 98; *Personal Knowledge,* 266–67, 303.

Let me close by stating my contention provocatively. I am proposing that there is no fundamental distinction between what we call scientific knowledge and what we call religious belief. While the objects of investigation are ontologically distinct, the epistemological process is remarkably similar, and if this were recognised then theological discussion would rightly regain its authority; if not as the queen of the sciences, then at least as an equal partner in the public and academic debate about what is real. For there simply is no chasm between knowledge and belief.

Chapter Four
The Authority of the Bible, the Flood Story, and Problematic Images of God

Terence E Fretheim

Many themes in the Scriptures would befit a conversation regarding biblical authority. I am particularly interested in the God who is presented in the Bible and issues of authority that have been raised by that portrayal, not least the association of that God with a remarkable range of problematic words and actions.[1] Such a concern is nothing new in the church; already in the second century Marcion had great difficulties with the Old Testament image of God, not least the divine anger and violence; indeed, he emerged with a truncated New Testament in order to rid it of any remnants of problematic Old Testament God talk. Practically speaking, Marcion has had many heirs. There has never been a time wherein the Bible did not create problems for the church in and through what it did say or did not say about God. These matters have been raised to new intensities in recent decades. My plan is to address this issue in and through questions raised by the biblical flood story and the God it presents.

Initially, let me offer a few words about biblical authority. My discussion assumes that the Bible is the word of God. In saying that, I understand that the Bible plays two roles. Most basically, the Bible has a formational or constitutive role in and through the work of the Holy Spirit. That is, the Bible has a unique capacity to mediate God's word of law and gospel, which can *effect* life and salvation for individuals and communities. Second, the Bible is the fundamental source for shaping and main-

---

1. For an analysis of the characteristics of the current context that have problematised issues relating to the authority of the Bible, see Terence E Fretheim and Karlfried Froehlich, *The Bible as Word of God in a Postmodern Age* (Minneapolis, MN: Fortress, 1998; Eugene, OR: Wipf and Stock, 2002) 81–7. I would emphasise even more strongly today that the Bible's own content creates problems for contemporary readers (for example, its violence).

taining Christian self-identity. We turn to the biblical books to discern (1) what the Christian faith was and essentially still is and (2) what the basic shape for Christian life in the world was and still essentially is. This claim grounds these reflections.

Persons with a shared high view of the Bible's authority have often disagreed over the interpretation of specific biblical texts and specific biblical issues (for example, infant baptism or free will). We know instinctively that the ascription of a high level of authority to the Bible does not guarantee the accuracy or truthfulness of our interpretations of texts (witness the Jehovah's Witnesses!). Indeed, a traditional viewpoint regarding the Bible's authority often issues in various interpretations of the texts, not least those regarding the depiction of God.

Again and again, the basic issue among interpreters is not the authority of the Bible, though the rhetoric may bend that way. The most basic issue is, rather, the authority given to a particular *interpretation* of the biblical texts, in this case, the God of those texts. That is, over the course of the interpretive process, some *interpretations* of specific biblical texts often *take on an authority that approximates the authority of the Bible itself.* Not uncommonly, if those interpretations are challenged, then the very authority of the Bible is thought to be called into question. This ascription of authority to *specific interpretations* of the texts often goes unrecognised and has, in and of itself, become a major problem in the theological and ethical discussions of texts. It is to the text itself that readers are *finally* held accountable, of course, however important a particular tradition or interpretation may be as a place to begin or to ground the interpretive process.

Let me complicate the matter from another perspective. People with a *low* view of the Bible's authority can have a highly *traditional* view regarding God. Indeed, basically similar perspectives regarding the God of the Bible can be held by orthodox Christians and those on the periphery of the church and even outside of the church altogether. Approach the average person on the street and inquire about their views of God; not uncommonly, many of those views will be remarkably similar to those held by traditional Christians. My experience with such individuals suggests that issues relating to the authority of the Bible are largely irrelevant when it comes to the conversation about the interpretation of theological matters in the Bible, including those regarding God.

Why is this the case? Some readers claim that theological interpretations of texts vary as much as they do because of differences in *the way the*

Bible is approached or used. This may be the case in individual instances, but the differences among us regarding the interpretation of God texts cannot be reduced to such a formula. Again and again, those who use the same methods of studying biblical texts (for example, the latest in historical or literary criticism) often come to different, indeed very different conclusions regarding the God of the texts. In other words, individuals who use essentially the same hermeneutic can sharply disagree with respect to the theological and ethical interpretation of the relevant texts.

Again, why is this the case? Most basically, our interpretations will often, perhaps always, be shaped significantly by more 'informal' matters. Bible interpreters are not blank slates when they read they Bible; they are deeply affected by what they have been taught and the broad range of their life experiences, including personal experience, communal and familial influence, and the churchly tradition within which they have been reared.[2] Something of 'who we are' as interpreters will inevitably be a part of any meaning we claim to see in a text.

Our personal convictions regarding God become deeply set over time and it often takes more than an exegetical insight, a theological treatise, or even a school of thought to dislodge them. Powerful personal factors are in play—often beyond our knowing—in the varying assessments we make of the textual and contextual evidence. This suggests that the most basic issue that undergirds interpreters' differences regarding the God they see in the texts has to do, not with biblical authority, but with the often *deep personal convictions* regarding God, formed over time, indeed a lifetime, which may be more or less deeply set within ourselves as interpreters, and have become central to what we understand our faith in God to be about. These more personal convictions will, in turn, lead back *to the level of authority we give to specific interpretations* of biblical texts, recognised or not.

This reality has been characteristic of all biblical interpretation through the centuries, though perhaps more sharply recognised in recent years. A key complicating factor in the present situation is that we have a more highly diverse group of biblical scholars and other serious readers than has been the case heretofore in the history of biblical interpretation (for example, female readers and third-world readers). This means, among other things, that a much more diverse personal experience is now at work when the text is being interpreted, not least theological interpretation. We

---

2. The church has long-held convictions regarding God that have been woven into confessional statements within the various traditions; this confessional linkage compounds the difficulty of breaking away from traditional interpretations.

should be more prepared to acknowledge the pervasiveness and depth of this reality.

As an example, the impact of the traditional churchly image of God has been considerable.[3] This churchly image of God includes such divine characteristics as these: omnipotence, omniscience, immutability, impassibility, atemporality. Though the Bible uses none of these words, their associated ideas have had an immense influence, consciously or unconsciously, on the way in which we interpret the word 'God' whenever we encounter it in the text. The result is that many of the actual biblical images for God have been neglected or harmonised to fit with these post-biblically formed divine attributes. This reality needs to be recognised before such problematic issues as divine violence can be fully considered. The common discussion regarding such issues with respect to the God of the Old Testament often assumes omnipotence and related claims; the extent to which that reality can direct the conversation needs forthright attention.

One of the ways in which we have sought to work with such difficult materials is through the time-honored rule-of-thumb for interpreting the Bible, namely, let Scripture interpret Scripture. That is, readers are called to interpret difficult texts in view of other, clearer texts. In more comprehensive terms, the entire Bible is to be taken into account in interpreting each verse. This interpretive process, however, helpful as it is, has its shortcomings, not as often recognised as they might be. For example, this hermeneutic has often proceeded in a harmonistic way so that the difficult issues are, finally, explained away. Such an approach tends to flatten out the Scriptures and does not recognise the evaluative dimension that is present across the texts themselves. For example, Scripture may well interpret itself *against* itself in view of the diversity of perspectives on any number of issues, even theological issues. We have often learned to work this way with, say, texts that reflect such social-order issues as slavery and patriarchy. That is, we lift up certain texts regarding freedom and equality (for example, Gal 3:28) and, rather than engaging in harmonistic efforts, have determined that such texts have priority and can be used to evaluate other texts. Generally speaking, theological diversity in the Bible should be allowed to stand rather than be harmonised; diversity is one of the great gifts that the Bible has to offer its readers, raising questions, sparking

---

3. I focus on the church, though comparable claims could be made with respect to Judaism.

the imagination, encouraging dialogue, and opening up the interpretive potential of the texts.

Needing attention in connection with this factor is what we might call a biblical centre, more traditionally called a canon within the canon. Every interpreter of the Bible has one, recognised or not. This centre is important for shaping our interpretations of the theology of a text, including statements about God. This centering reality is present already in the biblical text, which here and there draws certain claims about God into confessional statements. Hence, an inner-biblical warrant exists for thinking in terms of such a centre. Such confessions can be observed by (1) the nature of the genre that is present and (2) by their pervasiveness in the canonical witness to God. Two primary forms of this centering witness, and both are important, are historical recital (for example, Deut 26:5-9) and, particularly for our purposes, divine attributes (Exod 34:6-7, 'The Lord is gracious, merciful, slow to anger, and abounding in steadfast love and faithfulness . . . ').

That this latter credal genre was considered by Israel's theologians to be of special theological value is shown by the extent to which it is repeated across the canonical witness, both Old Testament and New Testament. Among other things, this repeated credal material shows that narrative is not enough, that story is insufficient. *What* you say about God is crucial, not just how you say it or how well you tell the story. These canonical witnesses commend an evaluative paradigm of making distinctions among texts regarding the nature of their place within the tradition and related issues of authority. This centering pattern continues in the New Testament, especially in its claim that the death and resurrection of Jesus is, to use the language of Paul in 1 Cor 15:3-4, 'of first importance'. It might also be noted that Jesus' statement about 'the weightier matters of the law' (Matt 23:23) or the 'greatest' of the commandments (Matt 22:38-40) continue in this tradition.

In sum, the kind of God confessed in the Old Testament credal formulations is the *kind* of God with whom Israel understands it has to do in every circumstance. This core testimony regarding God has an *authoritative* value within the Bible itself; that is, it constitutes an inner-biblical warrant for the evaluation of all biblical statements about God. At the same time, it is important to say that these statements do not shut down challenges to the confessional statements (for example, Jonah 4:2) or portrayals that stand in some tension with this centre (for example, Ps 77:4-10). Not everything that is said about God in the Old Testament can be harmonised.

To return to the traditional churchly claims about God of which we have spoken (for example, omnipotence, impassibility), it is remarkable that those theological claims seem at best tangentially correspondent with the centering witness about God that is present in the texts. The God in those credal statements is a deeply relational God—a key point—a perspective that seems not to centre at least some traditional churchly formulations regarding God.

I now consider a familiar text that seems to challenge many of the traditional descriptors of God, namely, the flood story in Gen 6:5-9:17. I would suggest that the placement of this narrative at the beginning of the Bible invites readers to read the rest of the Bible through the theological lens it provides. The image of God that we seek to develop here will affect how one reads other problematic texts regarding God.

God and the Story of the Flood[4]

A basic list of what God does in the flood story is remarkable: God expresses sorrow and regret; God judges, but does not want to; God goes beyond justice and decides to save some, including animals; God commits to the future of a less than perfect world; God is open to change and receptive to doing things in new ways in view of new divine experience with the world; and God promises never to do this again. Even more, the story witnesses to a God who acts in judging and saving ways beyond the walls of the chosen community. Indeed, in the larger creational context in which the flood story is embedded, God is the subject of a remarkable string of activities that are all too commonly reserved for the chosen community (by the chosen community!): God elects, reveals, saves from danger and death, and makes promises. And this is long before Abraham! And, the story suggests, long since Abraham. From the perspective of many a Bible reader, these are problematic images for God indeed—and commentators often move past them quickly. At the same time, they seem to be in tune with the theological centre of which we have spoken.

What might such language tell us about God? When all is said and done, this conversation will leave us with questions, but that in itself is an invitation to search for supporting texts and to engage in further reflection. Even more, I suggest that this language for God provides an im-

---

4. I assume basic historical and literary perspectives regarding this text and move immediately to theological considerations.

portant lens through which to read subsequent biblical descriptions of God, not least those of violence. The following ten points overlap with one another, but they deserve separate consideration and do not stand or fall together.

1. God uses agents in carrying out acts of judgment. It may be said that much, if not all of the violence associated with God in the Bible is due to God's decision to use agents that are capable of violence. Three dimensions of this issue in the flood story are important to consider:

a) God acts in and through the agents of storm and flood that actually do the destruction. Water and flood are the subjects of the key verbs that occasion the disaster (Gen 7:6, 10–12, 17–20, 24)

b) The created moral order (acts have consequences) is also an agent in and through which God works judgment. Indeed, it may be said that the agents of destruction emerge from within the very nature of the corrupt situation. The words for 'corruption' and 'destruction' (Gen 6:11–13) are from the same Hebrew root (*sht*); on a continuum, *sht* leads to *sht*. The same word is used to speak of human wickedness, the violence of 'all flesh', and its effects on the *earth*.[5] This language shows that the destructive agents are *intrinsically* related to human corruption and are *used* by God rather than being imposed by God from outside the dynamics of the situation.[6] Violence leads to violence. In other terms, creaturely violence has disastrous, indeed cosmic environmental effects (see, for example, Hos 4:1-3).[7] The words 'only', 'every', and 'continually' in 6:5 specify the depth and breadth of the sinful human condition, out of which grows the cosmic violence that follows.

c) God's agents in this situation also include a 'righteous' and 'blameless' Noah. He fulfills every divine command and his obedient human activity is sharply responsible for the salvation of a remnant of human beings and animals.

2. God repeatedly 'regrets' that God created humankind in the first place (Gen 6:6-7). God knows what might have been and profoundly de-

---

5. The phrase 'all flesh' includes animals (6:19; 7:15–16, 8:17), not least in view of 9:5, where animals are held accountable for taking the life of another; this may be a reference to carnivores, the eating of blood, as a violation of a vegetarian way of life.
6. It could be claimed that floods per se are *not* the effect of human violence; such natural events are an integral part of the world that God created. Rather, it is the range and intensity of the flood that is understood to grow out of human violence.
7. Sometimes God as subject stands in a prominent position (for example, Jer 19:7-9); in other texts, God's stance is more passive (for example, Hos 4:1-3), even withdrawing (Isa 64:6-7).

sires that things had not come to this! Here the past of God, what might have been, seems to stand in disjunction with the present of God, what actually is, and the collision of past and present in God occasions a deep divine regret and accompanying suffering. This point is also testimony to the temporality of God, who has so deeply entered into the life of the world that past, present, and future are real for God. This point regarding divine temporality has been seen already in God's resting on the seventh day of creation.

3. God's regret seems to assume that God did not know for sure that this would happen (as also in Gen 22:12; Deut 8:2). This does not mean that God is not omniscient, though some definitions of omniscience might be threatened by this understanding. The claim is still available that God knows all there is to know, including all possibilities, but there is a future which is not yet available for knowing, even for God.[8] Such language speaks against any position that God planned that the creation would take this course. What has happened to the creation is due most basically to creaturely activity, not divine. At the same time, God bears some responsibility for these developments by setting up the creation in such a way that it could go wrong, and could have such devastating effects. God created the world good, not perfect.

4. This regretful response of God assumes that humans have successfully resisted God's will for the creation. As such, this text is a witness to divine vulnerability in the unfolding creation. This is a God who takes risks, who makes the divine self vulnerable to the twists and turns of creational life, including human resistance. To speak of the resistibility of the will of God becomes a key for understanding many a biblical text that follows, not least the many passages that speak of divine anger. Why would God get angry if God's will were never successfully resisted?

5. God's initial reference to blotting out human beings seemed to allow for no exceptions (Gen 6:7), but God's pain and sorrow leads to a decision regarding Noah that changes that judgmental direction, with positive effects for 'all flesh'.[9] At the same time, importantly, this is not a change in

---

8. In thinking about God's power, it is often said that it is illogical to ask: can God make a rock so big that God cannot lift it? Comparably regarding God's knowledge, it is illogical to ask: Can God know a future which is not yet there to know?
9. Nothing that Noah has done is said to prompt Noah's finding favor with God. Yet, Noah's faithfulness is not just a blip on the cosmic screen, somehow irrelevant to God. Noah's walking with God counts with God; but it is understood to be a (not inevitable) consequence of God's prior action.

the character of God, but a change in divine strategy. This understanding of divine change suggests that the interpreter must speak of the mutability of God in some sense, albeit standing in the service of the divine immutability to be faithful and to act always in the best interests of the creation.

6. More generally, God is deeply and personally moved by what has happened to the relationship with humankind. In other words, this text is testimony to the affectability of God. God is herein revealed as one who is (deeply) affected by creatures both human and nonhuman (not just humans and not just Israel); God is not removed and detached from that world, but genuinely engaged with it and affected by that engagement.

7. More particularly, God grieves over what has happened to God's world (6:6-7). The NIV says it well, God's 'heart was filled with pain' (the same word used for the pain of the man and the woman in Gen 3:16-17). The basic character of the human heart in 6:5, 'every inclination of their hearts was only evil continually', is set alongside the disappointed and sorrow-filled divine heart (6:6). While the external and more objective picture in this story is one of disastrous judgment, the internal, subjective image is that of divine grief. To move to the judgment talk in the prophets, grief is what the God-ward side of judgment and wrath always looks like.[10] The image of God in the flood story is perhaps best described as that of a grieving and pained parent, distressed over what has happened to the human race (see Gen 6:5-7; compare Ps 78:40-41, Isa 63:7-10).

That divine judgment and divine tears go together has considerable theological import. Without the reference to divine tears, God would be much more removed and unmoved. Judgment accompanied by weeping, while still judgment, is different—in motivation and in the understanding of the relationship at stake. God's harsh words of judgment are not matched by an inner harshness. The strategy is to portray the kind of God with whom Israel, indeed the world, has to do, namely, a God for whom judgment is neither the first word nor the last. A word about such a God can be productive of hope. While God may give the people up to the effects of their sinfulness, God does not finally give up on them. In other terms, the circumstantial will of God in judgment is always in the service of the ultimate will of God to save.[11] To that end God can use judgmental

---

10. For detail, see Terence E Fretheim, 'Theological Reflections on the Wrath of God in the Old Testament', in *Horizons in Biblical Theology* 24 (2002): 1-26.
11. See Terence E Fretheim, 'Will of God in the OT', in the *Anchor Bible Dictionary*, volume VI, 914-20.

effects for a variety of positive purposes (refining, cleansing, insight, discipline).

The ethical implications of this understanding are considerable. If there were no *divine* judgment on sin/evil, then *human* judgment toward that which is oppressive and abusive would not carry the same weight. At the same time, if there were no sorrow associated with divine judgment, then human judgment would be given a freer range regarding harshness.

8. Such divine disappointment and grief over what has happened is revealing of a genuine divine relationship to the world.[12] God does not stand in a remote relationship to what has happened, like some divine mechanic seeking to fix the world from the outside. God personally involves the divine self in its brokenness and works on the situation from within (a move that Christians will understand as Christ-like). Human beings can now not be summarily stopped from sinning if the God-world relationship is to be honored.

9. Inasmuch as human beings are said to be just as sinful after the flood as before it (compare Gen 6:5 with 8:21), pain will be an ongoing reality for God. That is, the flood did not end the reason for the divine suffering. For God to continue to interact with this creation in the wake of such continuing creaturely defiance entails a divine decision to continue to live with such resisting creatures (not the response of your typical CEO!). This divine decision to go with a wicked world, come what may, means for God a continuing grieving of the heart. In other terms, the future of the creation that now becomes possible is rooted in this divine willingness to bear ongoing pain and sorrow. Indeed the everlasting, unconditional promise to Noah and all flesh *necessitates* divine suffering. That is to say, given the divine faithfulness to promises made, a pain-free future is not possible for God. For God to decide to endure a wicked world, while continuing to open up the divine heart to that world, means that God's initially expressed grief will be ongoing. God thus determines to take suffering into God's own self and bear it there for the sake of the future of the world. The world's future becomes dependent upon this divine suffering. It soon becomes clear that God is not simply resigned to evil or simply tolerant of human sin. But God must find a new way of dealing with the problem of sin and evil. And that way is the way of suffering and death. God's suf-

---

12. For detail regarding the centrality of relationship in Old Testament studies, see Terence E Fretheim, *God and World in the Old Testament: A Relational Theology of Creation* (Nashville: Abingdon, 2005), 13–22.

fering proves over time to be very powerful; indeed, it might be said that suffering is God's chief way of being powerful in the world.

10. This divine move leads finally to God's promises never to engage in such a destructive act again, repeated in 8:20–21 and 9:8–17. What do such promises mean for God? For God to promise not to do something ever again entails an eternal divine self-limitation regarding the exercise of both freedom and power. God thereby limits the divine options in dealing with evil in the life of the world—no more flood-like responses.[13] And, given the fact that God will be faithful and keep promises, does that not mean that divine self-limitation yields real limitation for God? God is capable of doing anything, but the certainty of God's faithfulness means that God cannot do so. The route of world annihilation has been set aside by God as a divine possibility. Divine judgment there will be (for example, Genesis 18-19), but it will be limited in scope. Sin and evil will be allowed to have their day and God will work from within such a world to redeem it, not overpower it from without. In spite of what people do, God will remain faithful. It is this *kind* of God with whom Israelite readers have to do, and it is primarily the word of divine commitment to promises made that they most need to hear.

In sum, what God does here '*recharacterises*' the divine relation to the world. God qualifies the workings of divine judgment and proceeds to promise an orderly cosmos for the continuation of life. God will never do this again! Only the language of change seems capable of describing what has occurred. God, whose character is unchangeable, is the one who has changed between the beginning and end of the flood, not human beings (although there are fewer of them around!). In view of God's experience with the world, God charts new directions in relating to that world.

These several characteristics of God are fundamentally in tune with the biblical centre of which we have spoken. It is this *kind* of God that provides a basic lens through which to interpret the God who is presented in all the biblical texts that follow.

God and Violence

If the Old Testament God can be characterised as being in a genuine relationship with the world such as we have described, might this help readers come to terms with other biblical texts that speak of violence, indeed

---

13. Except perhaps as a means to bring the world to an end?

divine violence? What difference might it make if one reads those texts of violence in and through these images of the flood story, not least those images wherein God places a limit on what God can do about violence? Indeed, is it not the case that such a re-characterised divine way with the world may issue in even more violence? By promising never to bring a violent world to an end, does not

God thereby open up that world to unending violence? From another angle, by loosening the divine control of the world (which the divine promise entails), God becomes even more closely associated with its violence, or at least potential for violence. How then might we articulate the divine association with violence in the post-flood world?[14]

To explore the ten matters above in detail would entail a major treatise. I focus on the first mentioned as a way of illustrating the task: God uses agents.[15]

The created moral order is such an agent. It might be defined as a complex, loose causal weave of act and consequence. That human sins of violence have consequences, including violence, is ongoing testimony to the *proper* functioning of the moral order, and this reality can be named the judgment of God. Just how God relates to the movement from sin to consequence is difficult to sort out, not least because the Old Testament does not speak with one voice about the matter.[16] But, generally speaking, the relationship between sin and consequence is conceived in intrinsic rather than forensic terms; that is, consequences grow out of the deed itself rather than being imposed from without as a penalty. As an example of the nature of God's involvement, see Ezek 22:31. God declares: 'I have consumed them with the fire of my wrath.' What that entails is immediately stated: 'I have returned [*natan*] their conduct upon their own heads.'[17] Notably, God does not (need to) introduce judgment into

---

14. See Terence E Fretheim, 'God and Violence in the Old Testament', in *Word & World* 24 (2004): 18–28.
15. For a helpful statement about agency issues in the Old Testament, see Frederick J Gaiser, '"To Whom Then Will You Compare Me?" Agency in Second Isaiah', in *Word & World* 19 (1999): 141–52.
16. For a recent effort, see Gene Tucker, 'Sin and "Judgment" in the Prophets', in *Problems in Biblical Theology: Essays in Honor of Rolf Knierim*, edited by H Sun et al. (Grand Rapids: Eerdmans, 1997), 373–88.
17. I have found over fifty Old Testament texts that link divine wrath with such formulations (for example, Ps 7:12–16; Isa 59:17–18; 64:5-9; Jer 6:ll, 19; 7:18–20; 21:12–14; 44:7–8; 50:24–25; Lam 3:64–66).

the situation; the destructive effects are already springing forth from the human deed.

While this understanding could be expressed in language such as 'your sins will find you out' or 'you reap what you sow' (Prov 22:8; Gal 6:7), Israel often, though not always (for example, Hos 4:1–3), explicitly linked God to the connection between sin and consequence. Interpreters have used several different formulations to speak of how God is involved: God midwifes, facilitates, sees to, puts in force, mediates, and completes the connection between sin and its effects. Whatever the language, such a move constitutes a giving of people over to the consequences of their own choices. Or, in terms of vocabulary usage, the same Hebrew word is used for the wicked deed and for the consequence of that deed, commonly translated 'disaster' (*ra'ah* leads to *ra'ah*; *'awon* leads to *'awon*). The judgment experienced flows out of their own wickedness, referencing the appropriate functioning of the moral order.[18]

The moral order, however, does not function in any mechanistic, precise, or inevitable way; it is not a tight causal weave. And so it may be that the wicked will prosper (Jer 12:1), at least for a time, and the innocent will suffer (Job) or get caught up in the effects of the sins of others (Israel in Egypt). Eccl 9:11, 'time and chance happen to them all', even introduces an element of randomness in relating human deeds to effects. One cannot therefore conclude that any experience of violence is due to that person's sin. Especially when working with communal violence, innocents (children, for example) may suffer deeply in view of the interconnectedness of the world. In the wake of the flood story, God, in at least a basic sense, has chosen to be subject to this just order and not to interrupt it or otherwise interfere with its functioning. (See Abraham's question in Gen 18:25, 'Shall not the Judge of all the earth do what is just?').[19] This divine involvement cannot be factored out, except to say that the looseness of the causal weave does allow God to be at work in the 'system' without violating or suspending it.

---

18. The understanding of *ra'ah* issuing in *ra'ah* may be observed in several formulations. God brings disaster (*ra'ah*), which is 'the fruit of *their* schemes' (Jer 6:19). Or, 'I will pour out *their* wickedness upon them' (Jer 14:16). Or, God gives to all 'according to their ways, according to the fruit of their doings' (Jer 17:10). Ezek 7:27 puts the matter in these terms: 'According to their own judgments I will judge them.' Like fruit, the consequence grows out of the deed itself. This leads to some correspondence thinking in the prophets; like produces like (for example, Jer 50:29); the people will stew in the juices they have prepared.
19. To use a cloth image, the moral order is more like burlap than silk.

In the functioning of the moral order, God is a genuine agent. But God always works in and through non-divine agents. People's sin generates snowballing effects; God is active in the interplay of sinful actions and their effects; 'third parties' are used by God as agents for that judgment (for example, Babylon).[20] We learn from the prophets especially that both God and God's agents (for example, Babylon under Nebuchadnezzar) are often the subject of the same destructive verbs.[21] In Jer 13:14, for example, God speaks: 'I will dash one against another, parents and children together, says the Lord. I will not pity or spare or have compassion when I destroy them.' In Jer 21:7, however, '[*Nebuchadnezzar*] shall strike them down with the edge of the sword; he shall not pity them or spare them or have compassion.' Again and again, the portrayal of God is *conformed to the agents God uses.*

Two specific texts may help make this point. One is Zech 1:15, where God says: 'I am extremely angry with the nations that are at ease, for while I was only a little angry, they made the disaster worse.' God was only 'a little angry'! The nations exceeded God's will for Israel and that misuse of power complicated God's merciful activity on Israel's behalf. God was not the only agent at work in the situation, as if God could at any time push a button and 'fix' matters. Hence, God's way into the future is not reduced to a simple divine decision to act. Because of God's committed relationship to the world, no resolution will be simple, even for God.

A remarkable number of prophetic texts speak of divine judgment on those nations that have been agents of God (Jer 25:12–14; 27:6–7; 50–51;

---

20. See Terence E Fretheim, *The Suffering of God; An Old Testament Perspective* (Philadelphia: Fortress, 1984), 77. This dynamic understanding of sin and its effects can also be observed in the use of the verb *paqad*, 'visit'. Its translation as 'punish' in NRSV is often problematic, as in Jer 21:14; 'I will punish you according to the fruit of your doings.' A more literal translation is more accurate: 'I will visit upon you the fruit of your doings' (see Jer 5:9; 14:10). It needs to be considered whether the word 'punish' is ever an appropriate translation of the verb *paqad* (see the related noun *pequdah*, often translated 'punishment', for example, Jer 46:21). See the formulation of Gerhard von Rad regarding Israel's 'synthetic view of life' and Israel's lack of punishment language in his *Old Testament Theology* (New York: Harper & Row, 1962), volume 1, 265, 385. The practical implications of the translation of *paqad* can be seen in a comparison of RSV and NRSV in Exod 20:5b. RSV translates 'visiting the iniquity of the fathers upon the children'; NRSV, however, changes that to read, 'punishing children for the iniquity of parents'. Strangely, the NRSV translates the same formulation in Exod 34:7 as 'visiting the iniquity of the fathers upon the children'.
21. For an extensive list, see Terence E Fretheim, *Jeremiah* (Macon: Smyth & Helwys, 2002), 36.

Isa 10:12-19; 47:1-15; Zech 1:15). Their excessiveness at the expense of Israel made the land an 'everlasting waste' (Jer 25:14).[22] The exercise of divine wrath against these nations demonstrates that they were not puppets in God's hand. They retained the power to make decisions and execute policies that flew in the face of the will of God; the God active in these events is not 'irresistible'.[23] God risks what the agents will do with the mandate they have been given. One element of that risk is that God's name will become associated with their excessive violence.[24]

Another text (Jer 42:10) reveals a divine regret: 'I am sorry for the disaster that I brought upon you.' God's response to Israel's suffering at the hands of overreaching agents is remarkable: 'I am sorry.'[25] How are we to understand this striking divine admission?[26] It appears that this divine response carries with it the sense of genuine regret; the judgment and its painful effects proved to be more severe than God had intended, or even thought they would be.[27] This direction for interpretation seems especially apt in view of the excessiveness of Babylon. Yet, God does not remove the divine self from responsibility for the use of means that resulted in an imperfect execution of the mandate. God, who does not foreknow absolutely what and how the agents will speak and act, accepts some responsibility for what has happened.[28]

This text reveals something of the inner life of God who uses agents that cannot be divinely controlled and is deeply pained at the results. God, however, is not bereft of resources to act in the midst of suffering. Indeed,

---

22. God's relationship to Babylon changes in view of its conduct as the agent of judgment. By its excessively destructive behaviors it opens itself up to reaping what it has sown (Jer 50:29; 51:24). God turns against God's own agent on the basis of issues of justice (see Exod 22:21-24). Such texts (cf. the oracles against the nations) assume that moral standards are known by the nations, to which they are held accountable.
23. Contrary to Walter Brueggemann, *A Commentary on Jeremiah: Exile and Homecoming* (Grand Rapids: Eerdmans, 1996), 222.
24. See John Sanders, *The God Who Risks: A Theology of Providence* (Downer's Grove, IL: InterVarsity, 1998).
25. The translation of *niham* is difficult (NRSV, 'be sorry'; NAB, 'regret' NIV/NEB, 'grieve'). Each of these translations carries the sense of a pained divine response to God's own actions.
26. See the discussion of William McKane, *A Critical and Exegetical Commentary on Jeremiah* (Edinburgh: T&T Clark, 1986), volume 2, 1033. For an earlier treatment of this and other texts, see Terence E Fretheim, "'I was only a little angry": Divine Violence in the Prophets', in *Interpretation* 58 (2004): 365-75.
27. For the idea the God thought something would occur, but did not, see Jer 3:7, 19-20.
28. On the issue of less than absolute divine foreknowledge, see Fretheim, *The Suffering of God*, 45-69.

suffering becomes a vehicle for divine action. God does not relate to suffering as a mechanic does to a car, seeking to 'fix it' from the outside. God enters deeply into the suffering human situation and works for the necessary healing *from within*. For God to so enter into the situation means that mourning will not be the last word.

In sum, these perspectives regarding agency are testimony to a fundamentally *relational* understanding of the way in which God acts in the world. There is an ordered freedom in the creation, a degree of openness and unpredictability, wherein God leaves room for genuine human decisions as agents exercise their God-given power. Even more, God gives them powers and responsibilities in such a way that *commits* God to a certain kind of relationship with them. This entails a divine constraint and restraint in the exercise of power in relation to these agents. God does not micromanage their activity, intervening to make sure every little thing is done correctly. And so an evaluation of the work of the agents may take this form: they overdid it! These texts are testimony to a divine sovereignty that gives power over to the created for the sake of a relationship of integrity. At the same time, this way of relating to people, not least the use of agents, reveals a divine vulnerability, for God opens the divine self up to hurt should things not go according to the divine will. And the actions of the agents often do go violently wrong, *despite* God's best efforts.

It may be said that God's most basic stance in the face of potential violence is nonviolence (see the divine offer in Jer 38:17–18). But, in order to accomplish God's work in the world, God may respond in and through potentially violent agents for the express purpose that sin and evil not go unchecked in the life of the world. In our reflections about such texts, we must certainly not set them aside just because they offend us; we must learn to read the Bible *against* ourselves, to let its texts be in our face. But, must we not also ask: is everything violent in the Bible that offends us appropriately offensive? One thinks of the absence of a condemnation of patriarchy or slavery, or the divine ordering of the wholesale slaughter of cities.

Might the Bible itself contain an internal evaluative process that could help us consider this issue? It is conceivable that the biblical centre of which we have spoken above could get us there, but that may not always be the case. Another way into this conversation is to note the extent to which key biblical characters raise questions about God and make challenges regarding God's (anticipated) actions. One thinks of Abraham's challenge to God in Gen 18:25, 'shall not the Judge of all the earth do what is just?' Or Moses in Exod 32:7–14, in the wake of the sin of the golden calf: Moses engages God with respect to the announced destruction of Israel, citing the tradition of the ancestral promises. God is responsive to human challenge and moves away from decisions made, in the case of Moses, or potentially so in the case of Abraham. These kinds of narrative testimonies invite Bible readers to engage in similar challenges to formulations regarding divine violence. This is no simple task; it is a major issue needing sustained dialogue and no satisfactory 'explanation' of this linkage of God and violence seems possible. Some summary considerations may help us grapple with the issues.

1. God works in and through human beings and other creaturely agents in the achievement of God's purposes for Israel and the world.

2. God does not perfect human beings, with all their foibles and flaws, before deciding to work in and through them. God works with what is available, including the institutions of society; among such institutions in that ancient context were certain ways of waging war and other trappings of government. More generally, violence will be associated with God's work in the world because, to a greater or lesser degree, violence is characteristic of the persons and institutions through which that work of God is done. And God does not micromanage their work, but exercises constraint and restraint. Thus such work by the agents will always have mixed results, and will be less than what would have happened had God chosen to act alone. Moreover, as we have seen, God does not necessarily confer a positive value on those means in and through which God works.

3. God's agents may exceed the divine mandate, going beyond anything that God intended. Notably, God assumes a share of the responsibility associated with that violence and takes part of the blame for using such agents.

4. Human beings, then or now, do not have a perfect perception of how they are to serve as God's agents in the world. While it is difficult to evaluate Israel's perception, it is important to note that the role of divine agents is often expressed in terms of the direct speech of God. Inasmuch as this is a phenomenon rare in the New Testament, should we understand that direct divine speech in the Old Testament in less than literal terms? Israel may have put into direct divine speech understandings they had gained through study and reflection rather than an actual hearing of God's words. And might we say that Israel did not always fully understand? Israelites did understand themselves to be the agents of divine judgment against,

say, Canaanite wickedness (Deut 9:4–5) and understood themselves to have received a word from God to that end. Did they fully understand?

5. That God would stoop to become involved in such human cruelties as war and other forms of violence is finally not a matter for despair, but of hope. God does not simply give people up to experience violence. Again and again, God takes the side of those entrapped in violence and its effects and does so in such a way that God himself, entering deeply into the life of the world, bears the violence in order to bring about good purposes. The tears of the people are fully recognised by God; their desperate situation is named for what it is. By so choosing to participate in their messy stories, God's own self takes the road of suffering and death. Because God suffers violence and the effects of violence, God thereby makes possible a non-violent future for the world.

Conclusion

Several considerations regarding the language of these texts seem in order by way of conclusion, with suggestions for further work.

1. These texts remind us of the inadequacy of all of our language about God. Every image comes up short; every metaphor has its 'No'; every textual reference to God stands in some discontinuity with the reality that is God. At the same time, it is important to remember that these images are not 'mere metaphors'; they have a great impact on our thinking, feeling, and being; willy-nilly, they will sink deep into our selves and shape us in ways beyond our knowing. It may be that certain images for God need to be set aside while retaining the 'yes' of which they speak in other terms; one thinks of indictment and judgment.[29]

2. By recognising these harsh images for what they are, they can keep us alert to the fact that language about God has powerful effects upon people and world, both positive and negative. Such language about God can be used to promote ideas and practices that do not serve life and well-being. We must not be casual or indifferent about our God language.

---

29. Erich Zenger's comment is helpful in thinking through such issues: '[T]he history of the impact and reception of an individual text in the annals of Judaism and Christianity must also be taken into consideration when we reflect on its revelatory character . . . [Some texts] can have been received in such a destructive way that the very knowledge of this negative history of reception becomes a constitutive part of the revelatory dimension of these texts.' *A God of Vengeance: Understanding the Psalms of Divine Wrath* (Louisville. KY: Westminster John Knox Press, 1996), 84.

3. Some would claim that violent language about God is designed to make readers uncomfortable, to show what their sin has wrought, and to reveal the depths of their own violence. To try to escape from the force of such texts is a typical sinner's response. But are there no limits to such an approach? It is one thing to be told that our sin has had incredibly negative effects upon the children of the world; it is another thing to say that God directly commands that such violence be visited upon the children. Such violent effects on children may at times be related to the complex issues of communal judgment and we are invited to think further about a God who is caught up in activities that so adversely affect children.

4. To engage texts of this kind could enhance our dialogical relationship with the biblical text more generally. The proper stance of readers in working with the text is not one of passivity or submission or simply listening. As with key figures such as Abraham and Moses, the word of God calls for genuine interaction.

5. By carefully considering the language and struggling with these texts, our imaginations may be sparked to seek ever more appropriate language for God. Certainly there are inadequacies in our present formulations that need attention, and these texts may not only remind us of this fact but may also serve to generate new reflections regarding God and the complexities of God's ways.

We return to issues of biblical authority. The various biblical developments that we have traced lead me to ask several questions: Do we need a high view of the authority of the Bible to be effectively about the theological interpretation of texts? Is the church wasting its time and energy being too defensive about the Bible, or even engaging in debates about its authority, especially when it seems not to affect the basic meanings we see in the text? The word we are called to bring to the world is not a word about the Bible and its authority. Any view of the Bible, or any use we make of the Bible, must be of such a nature that it doesn't detract from the hearing of the Word of God in and through these texts. Should we not then just proceed to preach and teach from biblical texts and let whatever esteem the Bible may have grow out of that encounter? This is a 'theology of the cross' approach to the Bible; that is, the Bible exemplifies its power in and through weakness. Would not such an approach to the Bible be more consistent with some of our most basic theological instincts?

Chapter Five
The Characterisation of God in Lamentations

Elizabeth Boase

One of the dominant characters within the book of Lamentations is God. God is spoken about and spoken to, although the voice of God is never heard. Various voices within the text speak of God, describing both God's actions and God's attributes. These descriptions give rise to various, and at times conflicting images: God is the violent destroyer of the city and her inhabitants; God is an absent God, whose presence is longed for; God is a God of steadfast love and mercy; God is the one in whom future hope lies. This essay analyses the multifaceted portrayal of the character of God as constructed in the book of Lamentations, exploring the implications of that characterisation for our understanding of the theology of Lamentations.[1]

The book of Lamentations is a problematic text. Written in the wake of the destruction of Jerusalem in 586 BCE these five poems give voice to the pain and suffering of the community. The images are bold and confronting, descriptive of the plight of the people, reflecting a strong sense of anguish, hurt, deprivation, anger, protest and also hope.

Among the most difficult images we encounter in the text are those that describe God. Within the poetry of Lamentations, God is spoken about and spoken to. Some of the images are comfortable—God as a God of steadfast love and righteousness, one in whom we should trust and hope. But alongside this image, in descriptions which are far more numerous and graphic, God is described as a violent oppressor who has wrought the destruction of the city and its people. God is also described as an absent

---

1. Thanks is given to the editors of *Australian Biblical Review*, where this essay appeared in 2008, for their agreement to its inclusion in this collection. The corrected version here was based on a paper originally presented at the *Hermeneutics and the Authority of Scripture* conference in 2007, mentioned in the Preface.

God, one who has withdrawn into silence, refusing to respond even when God's people call out.

The images we encounter concerning God are varied and at times contradictory. God is identified as the cause of the current suffering, but is also the only hope for the future. Given the tensions which exist in the characterisation of God, how are we to talk about God in relation to this text? Can we, or indeed should we, try to draw conclusions about the nature of God in light of the different characterisations?

This current essay explores the portrayal of God within Lamentations, followed by a discussion of the theological implications of the text. The exegesis is brought into conversation with Terence Fretheim's essay 'The Authority of the Bible and Imag(in)ing God'[2] in order to highlight my own hermeneutical position in relation to the tensions evident in Lamentations. Particular attention will be paid to the violent language used of God and its impact on our theology, concluding that within this text no one characterisation of God should be privileged. The text calls us into an engagement with the complexity of encountering God in the reality of lived experience, in the midst of pain and suffering.

The Characterisation of God in Lamentations

Within Lamentations the character of God is established through the speech of others. God is spoken about and spoken to. A variety of personae populate the text of Lamentations, each voicing their experiences.[3] The narrator (Lam 1:1-9b, 10-11b, 17; 2:1-20; 3:48-66; 4:1-16, 21-22), the personified city—Daughter Zion (1:9c, 11c-16, 18-22; 2:20-22), the community (3:42-47; 4:17-20; 5:1-22), and 'the man', a persona who appears in chapter three and is an intentionally gendered voice different from that of both the narrator and the feminine city (3:1-41). Each of these personae speak, voicing different aspects of the suffering, longing and hope experienced in the Jerusalem community in the wake of the destruction. There is no attempt to merge the variety of views expressed by the personae. The

---

2. Terence Fretheim, 'The Authority of the Bible and Imag(in)ing God' in *The Bible as Word of God in a Post Modern Age* edited by T Fretheim and K Froehlich (Minneapolis: Fortress, 1998), 112-26.
3. For the purposes of this essay, persona is defined as 'the mask of characterisation assumed by the poet as the medium through which he (*sic*) perceives and gives expression to his world.' (WF Lanahan, 'The Speaking Voice in the Book of Lamentations', in the *Journal of Biblical Literature* 93 (1974): 41-9 at 41).

multiple viewpoints sit alongside each other, leaving a sense of unresolved tension and rhetorical confusion.[4]

Alongside those who speak, various characters are spoken about. The narrator speaks of Zion, the community and of specific groups within the community. Zion speaks of herself, of the community as an entity, and of specific groups within the community—women, children, the elderly and so on. The man speaks primarily of his own suffering, but does address the community, and the community addresses its own pain, highlighting the plight of subgroups within its number.

Over and above this, however, each of the different personae speaks about God. God is one of the most dominant characters in the text, but unlike the personae, never speaks.[5] The absence of divine voice is significant. Although God is the subject of much of the speech, the divine silence means that no one description of God is authoritative, or in fact has more authority than any other. The audience engages with a multiplicity of viewpoints concerning God, but, in the absence of the divine voice, is not constrained to privilege one over another.[6]

Before examining the portrayals of God, it is important to consider the nature of this text as poetic. As poetry, Lamentations consists of a series of independent yet interrelated poems. Their essential character has been defined in terms of parataxis—the juxtaposition of poetic lines against each other—resulting in a seemingly haphazard movement between ideas

---

4. This understanding of Lamentations as a multivalent text has been highlighted in several recent publications, including Elizabeth C Boase, *The Fulfilment of Doom: The Dialogic Interaction Between the Book of Lamentations and the Pre-Exilic/Early Exilic Prophetic Literature* (LHBOTS 437) (New York: T&T Clark, 2006); FW Dobbs-Allsopp, *Lamentations* (IBC) (Louisville: John Knox, 2002); Kathleen M O'Connor, *Lamentations and the Tears of the World* (New York: Orbis, 2002).
5. Of the recent commentators, only Erhard Gerstenberger, *Psalms, Part, and Lamentations* (FOTL) (Grand Rapids: Eerdmans, 2001) finds the presence of the divine voice in Lamentations. He argues that, in 2:11–13, the divine voice is heard 'represented by an authorised speaker, entrusted to communicate God's personal involvement, pain and mercy'. I have argued elsewhere, however, that this is the voice of the narrator (*Fulfilment of Doom*, 219).
6. Narrative criticism identifies a hierarchy of authority with regard to biblical characterisation. The divine voice has ultimate authority, and the narrator's voice more authority than that of characters within a text: Robert Alter, *The Art of Biblical Narrative* (New York: Basic Books, 1981), 126; Shimon Bar-Efrat, *Narrative Art in the Bible* [(JSOTSS) (Sheffield: Almond Press, 1989), 64. Given that it is argued here that the author(s) of Lamentations have constructed various personae within the text, it is not assumed that one persona has more authority than another. The narrator is as much a construct of the text as the other persona.

and images.[7] This poetic form means that the characterisation of God is neither sustained nor logical in its development. Even where God is the focus of extended sections of text, there is a rapid shift of focus and change in reference. This is compounded by an absence of plot.[8] Actions are attributed to God, but these actions occur outside the framework of plot development, further emphasising the fragmentary development of character.

The current discussion focuses on three images, which are the most dominant and the most conflicting in Lamentations—God as the violent destroyer, God as absent, and God as a God of steadfast love and hope.

God as Violent Destroyer

This image of God as a violent destroyer is one of the most confronting in Lamentations. In varying degrees, three of the personae speak directly of God's violence: the narrator, the man, and Daughter Zion.

Both the narrator and the man have lengthy speeches that focus on God as the violent destroyer. In 2:1-9, the narrator describes God's actions against the city, focusing on the destruction of various aspects of the physical city (dwellings of Jacob, stronghold of daughter Judah [v 2], palaces and stronghold [v 5], wall of daughter Zion [v 8], gates and bars [v 9]) and of the cult (tabernacle, festival and sabbath, king and priest [v 6], altar and sanctuary [v 7]). There is little concern with the human impact of the destruction, although it is mentioned in verse 5 where God is described as multiplying mourning and lamentation.

Reference is made to God's anger and/or wrath six times (anger אַף [vv 1 (x2), 3 and 6], wrath עֶבְרָה [v 2], fury חֵמָה [v 4]) with verse 3 referring to God's fierce anger (בָּחֳרִי אַף) and verse 6 to the indignation of God's anger (בְּזַעַם אַפּוֹ). God is also described as acting without mercy (לֹא חָמַל [v 2]).

Over thirty verbs are attributed to God. Initially, the verbs emphasise God's elevated position. God has thrown down (שָׁלַךְ) from heaven the splendour of Israel. God breaks down (הָרַס), brings down (נָגַע), cuts down (גָּדַע). Verses 3-5 name God's failure to support the nation in the

---

7. Francis Landy, 'Lamentations', in *The Literary Guide to the Bible* (edited by Robert Alter and Frank Kermode; Cambridge: Harvard University Press, 1987), 329–34, at 330; see also Dobbs-Allsopp, *Lamentations*, 12–14.
8. Dobbs-Allsopp (*Lamentations*, 12–14) identifies that as lyric poetry, Lamentations lacks 'narrativising devices' such as plot.

face of the enemy, with God described as acting like an enemy (כאויב), destroying the city (בלע) and killing (הרג) the pride of the nation. These are holy war images, portraying the destruction of Jerusalem as a Day of Yahweh.[9]

Verses 6-8 intensify the destructiveness of God's actions, centring on the destruction of the cult. In verse 6 the verb חמס is used. The general sense is the wrongful application of violence, with the difficulty of this reading emphasised by its exclusion in the LXX and Syriac texts.[10] Verse 8 stresses the intentionality of God's actions, suggesting a sense of deliberation on God's behalf.

The audience is left with no doubt as to the agent or cause of the destruction. It is God who has brought about the devastation. The audience is overwhelmed by the sheer mass of violent verbs attributed to God. The relentlessness of the description is not broken by any sense of human responsibility. There is no reference to sin or transgression within this unit, although it could be argued that it is at least implied in the reference to God's anger (v 8: חשב יהוה להשחית 'Yahweh determined to lay in ruins').[11] It is, at best however, only implied.

A similar attribution of violence to God is found in the speech of the man in 3:1-18. In verse 1 the man identifies himself as the one who has seen affliction (אני הגבר ראה עני). In what follows, the man invokes images of physical violence against his body, much of it in the language of war (vv 5, 7, 11, 12, 13) and of hunting (v 11). The pursuit of the man is relentless, and he describes himself as physically and psychologically shattered (vv 17-18).

Zion also attributes violent action to God. Much of Zion's language is more personal and has to do with the pain and suffering God's actions have brought on her. As she breaks into extended speech for the first time

---

9. See Boase, *Fulfilment of Doom*, 131–4 for a full discussion.
10. See H Gottlieb, *A Study on the Text of Lamentations* (ACTA Jutlandica) (Aarhus: Aarhus University Press, 1978), 27.
11. Dobbs-Allsopp (*Lamentations,* 81) notes, 'such strong emphasis on anger imputes to God felt pain and a belief that that God has been wronged in a very serious way. And though such capacities elsewhere in the Bible are attributed to God, as biblical faith in general and Lamentations in particular steadfastly profess a God who is decisively impinged upon and affected by God's covenantal partners, they are not explicitly in evidence in this poem. That is, remarkably, nowhere in Lamentations 2 are we shown any sign of God's felt pain or of God having been wronged. Thus, God's anger, as shaped by the poem's rhetoric, becomes noticeably one-dimensional, almost solely the source for hurtful action, and leaving the poem's readership, then, with the impression, as O'Connor observes, of an "out of control" and "mad deity"'.

Zion identifies God as the cause of her suffering (1:12):

> Look and see if there is any sorrow like my sorrow,
> Which was brought upon (עלל) me, which the Lord inflicted (יגה) on the day of his fierce anger (חרון אפו).

Zion describes God as bringing sorrow and infliction, and as leaving her stunned (v 13). Zion also draws on war imagery (vv 13, 14, 18), but there is an underlying concern with the impact of God's actions against her as a person. Like the narrator and the man, Zion emphasises the fierce anger of God, and names the destruction as a day of God's anger (v 21).

The Absent God

Another dominant characterisation of God is as absent.[12] God's absence is portrayed in a number of different ways, and is voiced by all the personae.

---

12. There is little consensus in the literature with regard to the notion of divine absence, reflecting a tension in how it is that God can be understood to be absent. Walter Brueggemann discusses four pivotal texts (Ps 22:1; Lam 5:20; Isa 49:14 and Isa 54:7–8) in relation to God's abandoning activity. He suggests that there are five strategies evident in the literature which evade or dilute the presence of this motif in the Hebrew Bible: disregarding the texts; justifying God's action as a response to sin; arguing that God only 'appears' to be or is only perceived as absent (but is in reality still present); the positing of an absence in presence (ie, God is genuinely experienced as absent but that this experience contains within it "an assumption of cosmic, primordial presence, thus giving us a *dialectical notion of 'presence in absence' or 'absence in presence'* (29); and evolutionary supersessionism, which argues that both Israel's religion and in fact God 'developed' over time: 'Texts that Linger, Not Yet Overcome' in *Shall Not the Judge of All the Earth Do What is Right? Studies on the Nature of God in Tribute to James L. Crenshaw* edited by David Penchansky and Paul L Redditt (Winona Lake: Eisenbraun, 2000), 21–41. As we are drawing on the work of Fretheim, it is here worth noting his position with regard to divine absence. He argues not that God is absent from the people, but that the intensity of God's presence is, at times, diminished, that God has withdrawn an intensity of presence. He states, 'Thus while God's presence *to* Israel is diminished in intensity, God's presence *for* Israel remains alive and well in the world, though that may remain hidden from their eyes.' (Terence Fretheim, *The Suffering of God: An Old Testament Perspective* (OBT) (Philadelphia: Fortress, 1984), 66. As will be seen in the discussion which follows, although Israel does name an experience of God's absence, the very fact of voicing this experience to God still assumes an ongoing presence of God, or at least allows for the possibility of God hearing the cry. Despite this, for the voices within the text God has withdrawn and is for all intents and purposes absent from the people.

Chapter one opens with the words, 'how lonely sits the city' (הָעִיר אֵיכָה יָשְׁבָה בָדָד). Five times throughout the chapter reference is made to the lack of comforter for Zion, three times by the narrator (vv 2, 9, 17) and twice by Zion (vv 16, 21). While humans or other nations may qualify as comforters (vv 2, 12 and 19[?]), Zion herself seeks comfort from God as is evident in the pleas to God in verses 9, 11 and 20. Zion calls for God to 'look' (רְאֵה vv 9, 11, 20) and 'see' (נַבֵּט v 11).[13] The lack of God's seeing compounds the suffering which results from the physical destruction. The plea for God to look and see suggests that God is currently not looking, is not seeing – is absent. The current absence of God is held alongside the hope that God will again be present and alleviate the suffering.

The narrator's speech in chapter two, describes God destroying (שִׁחֵת) the tabernacle, abolishing (שִׁבָּה) festival and Sabbath, spurning (נָאַץ) king and priest (v 6), scorning (זָנַח) the alter in Jerusalem and disowning (נִאֵר) the sanctuary. These actions suggest that God has withdrawn from the temple, is no longer dwelling amongst the people.

Although God is said to have withdrawn from the people, in 2:18, the narrator exhorts Zion to bring supplications before the presence of the Lord: 'Cry aloud to the Lord! O wall of daughter Zion! Let tears stream down like a torrent day and night! Give yourself no rest, your eyes no respite!'[14] The God who has withdrawn is still the God before whom Zion must come to bring about a reversal of the current plight.[15]

The communal voice further names the divine absence. The man concludes his speech in 3:40–41 by turning to the community, exhorting them to confession: 'Let us test and examine our ways, and return to the

---

13. The same combination of verbs is used in an appeal to the passers-by in verse 12; however, they fail to qualify for the task.
14. The initial line of verse 18 is problematic and lengthy debate surrounds it. Despite much conjecture, there is little certainty as to the sense of this opening line. However, in the light of the remainder of verses 18–19, the line should be read as an imperative, calling on the city to lament: with B Albrektson, *Studies in the Text and Theology of Lamentations* (Lund: Gleerup, 1963), 116; Gottlieb, *Text of Lamentations*, 36; Iaian Provan, *Lamentations* (NCB) (Grand Rapids: Eerdmans, 1991), 75; Delbert R Hillers, *Lamentations* (AB 7A) (New York: Doubleday, 1992), 95; Claus Westermann, *Lamentations: Issues in Interpretation* (Minneapolis: Fortress, 1994), 143.
15. Samuel Balentine identifies that the cry of lament expresses the uncertainty of the suppliant. The suppliant gives voice to the reality of 'life lived in the period between what has happened in the past and what is hoped for in the future'. The experience of God's hiddenness is intensified by past experience and future hope of divine presence: *The Hidden God: The Hiding of the Face of God in the Old Testament* (Oxford: Oxford University Press, 1983), 166–7.

Lord. Let us lift up our hearts as well as our hands to God in heaven.' The community responds, 'we have transgressed and rebelled, and you have not forgiven (אתה לא סלחת)' (v 42). God is then described as being wrapped in anger (סכתה באף), in a cloud (בענן) so that 'no prayer can pass through (מעבור תפלה)' (vv 43-44).

Chapter three closes with an extended petition in masculine singular voice, calling on God to respond to the supplicant and to act against the enemy (vv 55-66).[16] Again—hope is found in the possibility of God's future presence, a contrast to the present absence.

The final chapter highlights the absence of God. Chapter five (v 1) opens with a petition to God to remember (זכר), look (נבט) and see (אר), emphasising the divine absence. Verse 20 asks if God has forgotten (שכח) the people completely, and why God has forsaken (עזב) them for many days. The closing of the chapter, and the book itself, raises the possibility that God may have permanently withdrawn:

> Restore us to yourself, O Lord,
> That we may be restored;
> Renew our days as of old—
> Unless you have utterly rejected us,
> And are angry with us beyond measure.[17]

The hopeful possibility of the appeal is negated by the final doubt-filled despair. The silence of God throughout the book becomes the central focus of the conclusion. God remains absent and silent.

---

16. The tenses within this unit are ambiguous, here translated in the precative voice. For a discussion of the issues see Iaian Provan, 'Past, Present and Future in Lamentations 3:52-66: The Case for the Precative Perfect Re-examined', in *Vetus Testamentum* 42 (1991): 164–74.

17. Lamentations 5:21-22. For discussion of 5:22 see Robert Gordis, 'The Conclusion to the Book of Lamentations (Critical Notes)', in the *Journal of Biblical Literature* 93 (1974): 289–93; Tod Linafelt, 'The Refusal of a Conclusion in the Book of Lamentations', in the *Journal of Biblical Literature* 120 (2001): 340–43. Linafelt's translation of the verse as a protasis without an apodosis—that is, 'an "if" with the "then" left unstated' (342)—captures the forward movement of the verse. He translates, 'For if truly you have rejected us, raging bitterly against us . . .'.

God as a God of Steadfast Love and Mercy

A third portrayal of God in Lamentations stands over and against the portrayals of the violent and absent God—God as a God of steadfast love and mercy. This view of God is implied by both the narrator and Zion in chapter one, but is most fully expressed by the man in chapter three, who moves from the genre of lament and complaint to a wisdom-like section which extols the virtues of God (3:21–39). This wisdom speech is often given privileged position when the theology of Lamentations is discussed, being seen as the highpoint of the book.[18]

The emphasis on God's justice and righteousness is seen initially in chapter one. Both the narrator and Zion make reference to the sin of the city and her inhabitants, implying that God's violent action was justified in light of this sin (1:5, 8, 14, 18, 22). Zion explicitly states, 'The Lord is in the right (צדיק), for I have rebelled against his word' (1:18), and in 1:22, Zion calls on God to deal with the enemy as God has dealt with her because of her transgressions. This linking of God's action as a justified response to sin is not, however, a sustained voice, with the sense of injustice emphasised through the sheer enormity of the suffering and the extent of the complaint.

The attribution of steadfast love and mercy is most strongly spoken by the man of chapter three. In a heavily didactic voice, the man reflects on the nature of God (vv 22–24, 34–39) and on the correct stance to be taken before God in the face of suffering (vv 25-30). Interspersed with this material are expressions of confidence that evoke the psalm traditions (vv 21, 31–33). The inclusion of this material introduces an element of hope otherwise absent from the book.

Having concluded the lengthy lament over his affliction, in verse 21 explicit hope is introduced by the man who states, 'this I call to mind, and therefore I have hope.' This hope lies in the recollection of God's attributes of steadfast love (חסד), mercy (רחם) and faithfulness (אמונה), attributes which are constant (vv 22-23).

Verses 25-30 define the attributes of God, who is good (טוב) to those who wait for him and to the soul who seeks him. Having counselled a

---

18. See, for example, Otto Plöger, *Die Klagelieder* (Tubingen: JCB Mohr, 1969), 128–29; Hans Jochen Boecker, *Klagelieder* (Zurich: Theologischer Verlag, 1985), 15–17; Joze Krašovec, 'The Source of Hope in Lamentations', in *Vetus Testamentum* 42 (1992): 221–33; Hans Joachim Kraus (cited Westermann, *Lamentations*, 35); Alan Mintz, 'The Rhetoric of Lamentations and the Representation of Catastrophe', in *Prooftexts* 2 (1982): 1–17; Hillers, *Lamentations*, 122.

patient waiting on God in the face of suffering, the man returns to an expression of confidence, again emphasising God's attribute of steadfast love (vv 31–33):

> For the Lord will not
>   reject for ever.
> Although he causes grief, he will have compassion
>   according to the abundance of his steadfast love;
> for he does not willingly afflict
>   or grieve anyone.

These verses do not deny the reality of the present situation, naming the rejection and grief as coming from God. The emphasis and hope, however, lies on the compassion (רחם) and steadfast love (חסד) of God. The remainder of the man's speech focuses on the justice of God, identifying that in the course of life both the good and the bad come from the hand of the Most High and again linking the present suffering with punishment for sin (vv 34–39).

Distinct hope is present within the speech of the man, based on the attributes of God's justice, love, righteousness and mercy.[19] It is in the recognition of these attributes that the man calls on the community to turn to God in confession (3:41–42). This hope filled position is, however, not maintained, with the community returning to lament genre, again naming the absence of God as their current experience.

The Characterisation of God in Lamentations

These three portrayals of God—God as a violent destroyer, God as absent and God as a God of steadfast love and mercy—are the most dominant in Lamentations. These images are conflicting and problematic, particularly the images of the violent and the absent God. The question then arises as to how we can move from the analysis of the text to using that analysis to inform our theology. How can we talk about God in light of the tensions

---

19. It is significant that in Lamentations there is no reference to God's past saving action as the basis of confidence in God. So also Fretheim who argues that the exile represents a gulf between past and future and that 'the hope of Israel is not to be placed in its own story, but in the kind of God whom it confesses' ('Imag(in)ing God', 121). Although Fretheim makes a relevant point here, my own reading diverges from his with regard to the weight given to the confessional statements present within Lamentations.

evident in Lamentations? Can we say anything coherent about the violent God who causes suffering and who is at the same time the God in whom hope for the future lies?

We cannot back away from the fact that there is a witness to the violence of God within the Hebrew scriptures. This witness occurs not only in poetic texts such as Lamentations, but is evident in a range of narrative texts.[20] The extent of the violence is particularly confronting in Lamentations as the discussion of God's violent action far outweighs the discussion of the motivation behind that action. While the sin of the people is named as one of the reasons for the destruction (1:5, 8, 9, 14, 18, 20; 2:14; 3:39, 42; 4:6, 13; 5:7,16), this is not a sustained argument. There is an emphasis on innocent suffering over deserved suffering.

In 'The Authority of the Bible and Imag(in)ing God', Fretheim suggests three areas to consider when evaluating the value of the God-talk which emerges from any given reading of a text.[21] These are:

- Point of view: ie, whose point of view is being expressed? Fretheim notes that there are three basic points of view concerning God within (narrative) texts—the narrator's, God's own self-talk and those of other characters. Of these, Fretheim places higher value on those of the narrator and God (noting, however, that God's self talk probably coincides with the view of the narrator).[22]
- Rhetorical purpose:
- The literary nature of the text.

---

20. See Ulrich Berges, 'The Violence of God in the Book of Lamentations', in *One Text, a Thousand Voices: Essays in Memory of Sjef van Tilborg* (edited by PC Counet and U Berges (Leiden: Brill, 2005), 21–44, especially 24–7, for discussion.
21. Fretheim, 'Imag(in)ing God', 115–17. Earlier in the essay, Fretheim asks, 'If some texts support traditional understandings, how does one work with these differences in any move to a biblical theology or a contemporary formulation? If there are not only multiple meanings of texts, but multiple theologies, do we let people just pick and chose the theology they like, and name it all biblical? But if we have a biblical theological pluralism, then the question of authority gets more complicated: are all such biblical theologies authoritative? Or are distinctions to be made among theologies? If so, does the Bible itself prioritise them? Are different biblical theologies pertinent for different times and places? Or is the authority of the Bible finally dependent upon its containing a univocal understanding of God?' (112–113).
22. 'Imag(in)ing God', 115.

These criteria provide a useful framework to begin our discussion. Although I am making use of his material, my own analysis diverges from Fretheim's in places, particularly with regard to using credal statements as a normative lens through which to read the text.

In terms of point of view, I have already highlighted that no one point of view is truly privileged in Lamentations. God's character is constructed by the personae in the text, but because God does not speak, divine authority is not given to any of those points of view.[23] In the history of interpretation, authority has been given to some of the personae over others.[24] The man of chapter three, who makes propositional statements about the character of God, is often seen as the voice which expresses the theological heart of the book. At other times, the narrator's voice is given precedence—especially where he identifies a causal link between God's action and Jerusalem's sin. Rarely is the feminine voice of the city given precedence.[25] I would argue, however, that this is a false move upon this text. All the voices are literary constructs, and all, at one point or another, characterise God in each of the images discussed. There is no privileged or authoritative voice.

In terms of rhetoric, that these poems are primarily lament must be taken seriously.[26] Their purpose is to give voice to the pain and suffering at the limits of experience, in the midst of an almost unimaginable crisis. All the structures that held the community together, political, social and religious, had been shattered. Meaning had collapsed, and the poems give

---

23. Against Fretheim, 'Imag(in)ing God', 115. In relation to Lamentations, the narrator has no more authority than the other personae in the text. All the speaking voices within this text are personae, constructed to give voice to multiple viewpoints on the destruction.
24. See note 18 above.
25. An example of the undervaluing of the feminine voice is found in the work of Mintz. He states, 'To deal with this threatened loss of meaning—what amounts to a threat of caprice, gratuitousness, absurdity—Zion as a figure is simply not sufficient; a woman's voice, according to the cultural code of Lamentations, can achieve expressivity but not reflection. And now acts of reasoning and cognition are the necessary equipment for undertaking the desperate project of understanding the meaning of what has happened. The solution is the invention of a new, male figure, the speaker of chapter 3 . . . whose preference for theologising rather than weeping is demonstrated throughout' ('Rhetoric of Lamentations', 9).
26. Fretheim raises the issue of the authority of lament texts when he asks, 'What about the theology of, say, the lament psalms? Inasmuch as they are spoken in situations of deep distress, is their understanding of God comparable to what moderns might say in a tight spot, but would never say in a carefully formulated statement?' ('Imag(in)ing God', 116).

strong voice to the resultant confusion. These poems are not carefully formulated statements, are not systematic doctrines, are not reflections on the ontological nature of the divine, but the pouring out of human experience.[27] The poems tell us of the experience of God, but do not tell us all there is to know about God.

In his discussion Fretheim argues that we need to consider the literary nature of the texts we are dealing with, and in particular that biblical characters, here God, are literary constructs. Fretheim suggests that there are two dictums which need to be avoided when talking about the character of God on the basis of biblical texts. One is that we identify the real God with the God who is embodied in the text—ie, by suggesting that God does not transcend the text. The God of the text is a metaphorical God, and as metaphor, we are called to question the is and the is not—the yes and the no—of the representation. The text calls us to engage with the portrayal, but not to assume that this text, or any text, says all there is to say about God.[28] Lamentations itself opens us up to this type of engagement. We have seen that the characterisation of God is not univocal. God is both the problem and the solution, is consecutively a violent presence, an absent figure and a God of steadfast love. The very nature of the text draws us into a dialogic interaction, shifting our focus constantly between different experiences of God, but never finally concluding or validating one over another.[29]

While we need to avoid the trap of equating the actual God with the textual God, we equally need to avoid completely dissociating the textual and the actual God. While God may transcend the text, God is still mediated through the text.[30] In the case of Lamentations, that includes the God

---

27. Claus Westermann argues that within lament 'the sufferers are encountering something about God which they cannot comprehend and that they have reached the limits of their own intellectual capacity. The sense of awe before the majesty of God prevents any attempt at rationalisation.' "The Complaint Against God", in *God in the Fray: A Tribute to Walter Brueggemann*, edited by T Linafelt and TK Beal (Minneapolis: Fortress, 1998), 233–41 at 239.
28. 'Imag(in)ing God', 117; so also Dobbs-Allsopp, *Lamentations*, 45.
29. Dianne Bergant states that the Israelite 'religious language was imaginative and paradoxical, attesting to personal experiences of God and using whatever forms best communicated the revelatory character of that experience. Its metaphorical character continues to open us to possibilities of expansion and insight that precise philosophical or descriptive discourse cannot provide. It generates impressions rather than propositions.' 'Violence of God: A Bible Study', in *Missiology: An International Review* 20 (1992): 45–54 at 46.
30. 'Imag(in)ing God', 117–18.

of violence who is experienced as one and the same God as the God of steadfast love and mercy. As audience, we need to look beyond the text to the God who transcends the text, but also mediate God through the witness of text. God both is and is not the character portrayed, includes but is not limited to the characterisation.

But again, we are left with the question of mediating between the different characterisations of God within this specific text. Even if we identify the metaphoric nature of God's characterisation, do we, or should we give more weight to one image over another.

Fretheim would, perhaps, argue that yes, we should. In dealing with the issue of characterising God, Fretheim calls for the recourse to confessional claims about the character of God as a hermeneutic guide in mediating between differing portrayals. He argues that we can identify credal statements such as that found in Exodus 34:6–7 as a ruling metaphor.[31]

> The LORD, the LORD,
> a God merciful and gracious,
> slow to anger,
> and abounding in steadfast love and faithfulness,
> keeping steadfast love for the thousandth generation,
> forgiving iniquity and transgression and sin,
> yet by no means clearing the guilty.

This metaphor of God, this image, is pervasive and reflects well the tradition. In addition, it occurs in a credal or confessional statement that has 'high value' for the community of faith. Essentially, these credal like statements are propositional not experiential. While this confessional statement may have its roots in the experience of Israel's history, with its essence drawn from salvation history, this truth claim cannot be reduced simply to the narrative of God's salvific acts. The confession focuses on the nature of God not the action of God. While the narrative of Israel's history may describe the God who saves, the narrative alone does not tell us about the *type* of God who saves. The truth claim moves beyond the experiential to the propositional, and Fretheim would argue that all portrayals of God should be read through the filter of this truth claim, in this way delimiting the possibilities of meaning when we move from the characterisation of God in the text to theological claims about God.[32]

---

31. 'Imag(in)ing God', 120.
32. 'Imag(in)ing God', 121–22. Fretheim in fact draws on Lam 3:20–32 to support his ar-

But is this valid for Lamentations? Should we limit the value of the different and contradictory characterisations by filtering the difficult ones of God's violence and God's absence through the image of the God of steadfast love? If so, the voice of the man who expresses hope on the basis of the steadfast love and mercy of God is the voice that should be privileged, as has happened in the past. It is this voice that opens the door to future hope in Lamentations and it is this confessional statement that allows the contrasting views of God to be held together within the confines of this text.

While this hermeneutic move may well allow the different voices to be held together, we need to be very careful in taking this step, because to do so actually denies the nature of the text itself. Theologically and propositionally, we may want to draw certain claims about God from Lamentations, but that is our concern not the text's. Lamentations resists this type of interpretation. We need to take seriously the genre of the text as primarily lament and allow the expressions of pain and anguish to be voiced without trying to reduce them down to propositional statements about God. Lamentations is not propositional; it is experiential and for Israel, at this time in her history, God was contradictory. God was both problem and solution, violent, absent and the longed-for future hope.[33] The text invites us to grapple with these different experiences of God, not necessarily asserting that one experience is universally and always true, or even propositionally valid. That is not the purpose of the text. The text is an invitation to engagement with the complexity of experiencing God in the reality of lived experience, in the midst of pain and suffering. It is an

---

gument. He states, 'The God confessed by Israel remains constant across the story's interruptions, especially the chasm of the exile. The book of Lamentations, which never appeals to God's actions in Israel's past, makes this kind of confession (3:20-32). In the midst of the great gulf between past and future, the hope of Israel is not to be placed in its own story, but in the kind of God whom it confesses. Hence, the God who is the subject of sentences in the narrative is to be understood fundamentally in terms of those generalisations.' A differently nuanced understanding of this section of text is articulated by Berges who states, 'The biblical protest against Jhwh, who acts in contradiction to his own ethical standards, is not rooted in a cultural disapproval of a violent God, but in a hope to experience his benevolence again. The sapiential reflection of the geber in the center of Book of Lamentation (3:22-24), does not present the solution to the problem of divine negativity, but the internal motivation to protest against it.' 'Violence of God', 41–42. This reading of Berges, it seems, allows the voice of protest to maintain its integrity.

33. Berges (41) argues that, 'the wisdom-inspired reflection of the *geber* in Lam 3 leads into the right direction, ie, "to hold and affirm conflicting and contradictory truths without eventually surrendering either"', (citing Dobbs-Allsopp, *Lamentations*, 120).

invitation to a dialogue that ends on a question, leaving hope only in the possibility of finally hearing a response from the God who is silent.

Chapter Six
The Reappropriation of the 'Old' Testament as the Key to Hermeneutical and Ecclesial Renewal

Ockert S Meyer

Although the church's designation of the Hebrew Scriptures as 'Old' Testament was unfortunate, it was nevertheless from the beginning accepted as a part of the biblical canon, albeit not always by everyone and with the same enthusiasm. However, more unfortunate than the mere name of 'Old' Testament[1] had been the church's reluctance to allow Judaism, via the OT, to help shape her biblical hermeneutics. This has had important consequences for the way biblical authority and hermeneutics have been taught and understood. It can even be argued that what often amounts to the eclipse of the OT in practical congregational teaching and worship contributed substantially to the rise of biblical fundamentalism since the Enlightenment as well as a modern day gnosticism in more recent times.

It was in the twentieth century that a number of Christian theologians (among others Bonhoeffer and Miskotte) have come to realise the importance of the OT, both in terms of biblical hermeneutics, as well as in countering the wave of secularism and its profound impact on the post Enlightenment church.

In this paper I would like to explore this role of the OT, as well as the role contemporary Jewish theologians (with special reference to Abraham Joshua Heschel) and Judaism can play in this endeavour.

It is certainly true to say that the Church[2] has had an ambivalent relationship with the Jewish scriptures. In spite of the fact that its acceptance had been reiterated and confirmed time and time again by the major coun-

---
1. Hereinafter OT will be used for 'Old' Testament.
2. When I refer to the 'Church' in this essay, I speak from a specific situation, namely my experiences within the Uniting Church of Australia, but I have the worldwide Christian church in mind. The issues touched upon here concern not only certain denominations but the catholic church.

cils of the church, there have always been voices opposing it, denouncing it and ultimately rejecting it.

In his struggle against Marcion and Gnosticism, the second century Irenaeus, had been one of the early voices to come out in support of the OT. However, except for him and the later Reformed tradition, as the Dutch theologian, Hendrikus Berkhof points out, there had been little systematic interest in what, he calls 'the way of Israel'.[3]

Hence it is not surprising that since the demise of the Marcionite church in the fourth century, Marcion's anti-OT teachings have always managed to find fertile ground in the Church, albeit in different forms and for different reasons. Adolf von Harnack provides a well-known example. In his *Marcion, das Evangelium von fremden Gott* he commented,

> to reject the OT in the second century was an error that the church rightly resisted; to maintain it in the sixteenth century was a destiny the Reformation could not escape; but still to preserve it in the nineteenth century as one of the canonical documents of Protestantism is the result of religious and ecclesiastical paralysis.[4]

The idea that Harnack expresses here may very well be the best and most succinct summary of the situation today. For in the contemporary Church the OT is perhaps not so much regarded as something which needs to be opposed, but much rather as something which has become overtaken by time and can therefore rightly be ignored.

It is my contention in this paper that the hermeneutical vacuum left by the *de facto*[5] disappearance of the OT played a significant role, both in the growth of fundamentalism, as well as the subsequent crisis of ethics, as it was exposed among others in the sexuality debates in various denominations.

---

3. H Berkhof, *Christian Faith. An introduction to the study of the faith*. (Grand Rapids: Eerdmans, 1979), 224. According to Berkhof this changed later in the twentieth century, when a number of theologians, from various denominational backgrounds have taken an interest in the OT and Judaism.
4. Quoted from Berkhof, *Christian Faith*, 223.
5. I use this term because there is no formal rejection of the OT in the church. It is still included in the lectionary readings of almost every denomination. However in practise, and apart from liturgical references, it receives marginal interest in terms of preaching. A regular churchgoer in the UCA has told me that he has not heard a sermon from the OT for a number of years.

Commensurate with the backseat role of the OT, but much more widespread and pervasive in its consequences was the lack of interest and often the ignorance of Jewish theology in the Church. Until the late twentieth century, very few theologians took Jewish theology seriously.

One notable exception was the Dutch theologian, KH Miskotte (1894–1976). During a visit to a book market in Cologne, Germany, he discovered Franz Rosenzweig's (1886–1929) monumental work, *Stern der Erlösung*.[6] It was Rosenzweig who opened Miskotte's eyes, not only to the Jewish Scriptures as such, but also and perhaps even more importantly to the *Jewish* understanding of Revelation and the subsequent structure of Scripture.

The ineffable Name

What Miskotte learnt from Rosenzweig and Judaism in general, was that in biblical theology, everything depends on the ineffable Name. In claiming this, he is not proposing a particular dogmatic approach but rather pointing to an order or sequence that rests in the structural witness of Scripture and especially in the living world of the Old Testament. The *Tanakh* is structurally different in the sense that its point of departure is not the seeking human, but the human being who knows him or herself to be seen, to be found.

This notion underpins every attempt to understand the Jewish Scriptures. In the incomparable description of Rabbi Abraham Joshua Heschel:

> The Bible is primarily not man's vision of God but God's vision of man. The Bible is not man's theology but God's anthropology, dealing with man and what He asks of him rather than the nature of God . . . In the depth of our trembling,

---

6. English translation, *The Star of Redemption* (Beacon Press: Boston, 1964). What concerned Rosenzweig was the alienation of religion and life, of synagogue and world, of Word and World and he considered it his vocation to mend this rift. The way he chose to do this, his 'new thinking', required a break from German Idealism, a thinking that 'ensconces common sense in the place of abstract, conceptual philosophising, posits the validity of the concrete, individual human being over that of "humanity" in general, thinking that takes time seriously, fuses philosophy and theology . . . ' (NN Glatzer in the preface to *The Star of Redemption*, xiv). In short, Rosenzweig attempted to do this by demonstrating that the three concepts of thought—God, World and Man—cannot be deduced from one another, that these are primary forms that underlie reality, but that they at the same time inter-related.

all that we can utter is the awareness of our being known to God. Man cannot see God, but man can be seen by God. He is not the subject of discovery but the subject of revelation.[7]

Both historically and epistemologically this is of crucial importance. Historically we have to understand that Israel worshipped God as a god among the gods[8] but at the same time as a god totally different from the gods. This difference is not based on human discernment but in the Name and in the Self-revelation of the Name.

This Self-revelation[9] is found in Exodus 3:14 'I am who I am'. Hence we can say, JHWH is both a proper name ánd a nameless Name. JHWH is a proper name because everything depends on Gods tangible self-distinguishing in the world of the gods. At the same time JHWH is a nameless name because God frees God-self from all human control.[10]

This brings us to the epistemological mystery regarding the Name: God is cognisable, not on account of God's divinity but on account of God's earthly presence. Knowledge of God is mediated through God's virtues,[11] not by means of God's eternal being.

The biblical epistemological centre is: JHWH is Elohim! (Not Elohim is JHWH.) Hereby the nameless Name creates a certain epistemological sequence, a sequence that marks and determines all biblical theology. The reverse order is untenable because that presupposes knowledge of the Name preceding the Self-revelation.

Hence we can say in the Torah as holy teaching, a specific sequence is established, an epistemological sequence that always moves from the particular to the general. Corresponding with this epistemological sequence is the structure of the Tanakh itself, whereby the Torah as the witness to

---

7. AJ Heschel, *Man is not alone. A Philosophy of religion* (New York: Farrar, Straus and Giroux, 1951), 129.
8. KH Miskotte, *Edda en Thora. Een vergelijking van germaansche en Israëlitische religie.* (Kampen: JH Kok, 1983), 29.
9. Abraham Heschel points out that Judaism would never use the term 'Self-revelation' of God. In Judaism God does not reveal God-self; God only reveals God's ways.
10. In the ancient world, the giving of names was a way of exerting control over those named subjects. Compare for example the narrative of Genesis 1 where the humans name the animals.
11. Instead of the usual 'attributes' of God, Miskotte prefers to talk about God's virtues. Levinas reminds us that the attributes of God are not given in the indicative, but in the imperative: 'The knowledge of God comes to us like a commandment ... To know God is to know what must be done.' E Levinas, *Difficult Freedom. Essays on Judaism.* (Baltimore: The Johns Hopkins University Press, 1990), 17.

God's immediate involvement forms the basis of the Tanakh. Only on a next level are the prophetic books (as the interpretation and application of the Torah) and on a third level the Writings (as the human response to the law and covenant).

The significance and importance of such a hierarchical structure is that the unity of the Hebrew Scriptures is not regarded as the unity of a particular codex, but the unity of God's concern, the unity of God's holy presence. In this regard Miskotte likes to speak of the OT's *plus*,[12] namely that it contains the Torah, the *Deus praesens*, the revelation of the One who acts and speaks. At the same time this means that law and ethos are shaped and formed, not so much by jurisprudence, but is much rather derived from and a result of a living relationship based on the *Deus praesens*.

This view makes it possible to view the unity of the Scriptures from a different perspective than the usual promise-fulfilment model. The NT is not the fulfilment of the OT, but God's work through Jesus Christ is—an event to which both New and Old Testaments testify. A much better way, according to Miskotte, of expressing the relationship of the two Testaments is to say that the witness of the OT relates to the time of anticipation and the witness of the NT to the time of remembrance. And as such both refer to the same Event.[13] This 'Event' is God's action in Jesus Christ; it is the living God acting on the stage of history; uttering the Name, the ineffable Name, whereby life is mediated in all its fullness.

This relates very much to the central thought of Judaism which is not to be found in the Torah, no matter how holy it is. 'The central thought of Judaism is *the living God*.'[14] According to Abraham Heschel there are two sources which make access to this mystery possible: memory (tradition) and personal insight. In other words, sensing, experiencing, knowing the Name can only be achieved in relation to two other things. These two are the Word and the world. The Name points us to the Word and to the world. In saying this, it is asserted that neither faith in the literal Word nor faith in literary science will suffice.

---

12. 'tegoed' is the Dutch word. It is very hard to translate to English. In a financial context it can refer to credit or an asset, but it can also be the valuable aspect of something. In the way it is used here, it refers to the 'added value' of the OT, hence 'plus'.
13. KH Miskotte, *Als de goden zwijgen. Over het zin van het Oude Testament* (ET: *When the gods are silent*) (Kampen: JH Kok, 1956), 93. 'Het getuigenis van het Oude Testament voltrekt zich in de tijd-der-verwachting en dat van het Nieuwe Testament in de tijd-der-herinnering. Beide zijn relatief ten aanzien van de tijd der Openbaring zelve.'
14. AJ Heschel, *Between God and man. An interpretation of Judaism.* (New York: Simon & Schuster, 1959), 242.

Whereas Christian hermeneutics have tried to find a way between these two, between Word and World, and therefore engaging in a perpetual struggle to preserve the integrity of both, Judaism points us to a different level, a different plane of understanding.

> In our encounter with the Bible we may take either a fundamentalist attitude which regards every word as literally valid, making no distinction between the eternal and the temporal, and allowing no place for personal or historic understanding, or for the voice of the conscience. Or we may take a rationalist attitude which, taking science as the touchstone of religion, regards Scripture as a poetic product or myth, useful to men of an inferior civilisation and therefore outdated at any later period of history.
>
> Philosophy of religion has to carry on a battle on two fronts, trying to winnow false notions of the fundamentalist, and to dampen the over-confidence of the rationalists. The ultimate task is to lead us to a higher plane of knowledge and experience, to attachment through understanding.[15]

Name and Word

It is impossible not to note the exulted tone which Judaism employs when she refers to the conception of the Torah. It is indeed the type of language that would trigger every possible fundamentalist-detector in Christianity. And yet at the same time it is this very language that makes fundamentalism an impossible option.

To understand this, we have to bear in mind that the Torah is used in two senses: in the first place, there is the supernatural Torah that precedes the creation of the world and secondly, there is the revealed Torah.

Corresponding with these two is the dual tradition of the Oral and the Written Torah. According to one midrash[16] Moses received two Torahs on Mount Sinai: the written Torah which God dictated to Moses during the day and the oral Torah which God explained to him during the night.[17]

---

15. AJ Heschel, *God in search of man. A philosophy of Judaism.* (New York: Harper & Row, 1955), 272.
16. A midrash is an individual rabbinic legend.
17. H Schwartz, *Reimagining the Bible. The storytelling of the Rabbis.* (New York: Oxford University Press, 1998), 3.

It was exactly this, as Howard Schwarz[18] points out, that allowed the rabbis to, on the one hand, embellish, retell, reimagine, or even radically change the stories of the Torah and on the other hand, maintain that the Torah was dictated by God to Moses and that therefore every word and every letter, yes even the crowns of the letters were meaningful and contained all truth.

In other words, even if the Torah was dictated by God, it can never lay any claims upon being the complete Torah. What God has given, must be refined and completed by humankind.

> Thus Judaism is based upon a minimum of revelation and a maximum of interpretation, upon the will of God and upon the understanding of Israel . . . The bible is the seed, God is the sun, but we are the soil. Every generation is expected to bring forth new understanding and new realisation. The word is the word of God, and its understanding He gave unto man.

And most crucially:

> The source of authority is not the word as given in the text but Israel's understanding of the text. At Sinai we received both the word and the spirit to understand the word.[19]

Heschel continues to argue that even though the words of Scripture are the only lasting record of what was conveyed to the prophets, they are neither identical with nor even an adequate rendering of divine wisdom. It is in this context that the phrase the 'word of God' is made intelligible. This can never refer to the word as a sound or a combination of words, for whatever reached the ear of the prophets can never be identical with the uttering of God's Spirit.[20] In other words, the prophet is touched by the Spirit, receives the idea from the Spirit, but the way he expresses this, is his choice of words.

---

18. Schwartz, 3.
19. Heschel, *Between God and man*, 248.
20. Heschel, *Between God and man*, 245. 'Israel could not possibly have received the Torah as it came forth from the mouth of the Lord, for the word of the Lord is fire and the Lord is a fire that consumes fire.' (246).

This doesn't mean that the Bible is *less* than the word of God; it is *more* than the word of God: it is the word of God *and* man.[21] In fact, Heschel says that the great mistake of dogmatic theology has been its insistence on the *objective* revelational character of the bible. This has not only opened the door to a fundamentalist understanding of the bible but has indeed exposed the Church to the very real threat of bible-worship.[22]

However, having said that, the charge from Christianity over the years and especially in our time, against what can be described as a co-revelational[23] approach to the Bible, is one of subjectivism and relativism. To this charge Heschel responds in the following way:

> Israel's understanding of the word was not cheaply or idyllically won. It was acquired at the price of millennia of wrestling, of endurance and bitter ordeals of a stubborn people, of unparalleled martyrdom and self-sacrifice of men, women and children, of loyalty, love and constant study ... Without our continuous striving for understanding, the Bible is like paper money without security. Yet such understanding requires austere discipline and can only be achieved in attachment and dedication, in retaining and reliving the original understanding as expressed by the prophets and the ancient sages.[24]

Two important aspects of Jewish hermeneutics have emerged here. The first one relates to the fact that not the Scriptural text, but Israel's interpretation, is regarded as the source of authority. This means that understanding is not a matter of the distilment of a certain moral or abstract principle from the text, but indeed a completion of the lives of those whom the text

---

21. Heschel, *God in search of man*, 260.
22. It is fascinating to see how well Judaism understands this problem and how it was dealt with, already by the early rabbis. In reflecting on the story of the golden calf in the bible, Svi Kolitz suggests that Moses broke the tablets of the Law, not because he was angry, but because he realised the very real danger of the Jews worshipping the Tablets of the Law. When Moses, on his return from the mountain found the people in a frenzied, idolatrous mood, he was seized by the fear that the Tablets could be worshipped, not only *apart* from God, but indeed *against* God: S Kolitz, *The Teacher. An existential approach to the Bible*. (London: Jason Aronson Inc, 1995), 176.
23. Heschel, *God in search of man*, 260.
24. Heschel, *Between God and man*, 248.

bears witness to. It involves going into the 'word-world'[25] of the bible and becoming part of the lives of our spiritual ancestors.

Miskotte understood this very well when he said that the Church is not supposed to articulate a new philosophy of life *on the basis of the bible*, but is indeed invited into the living environment, into the word-world of the bible. It is going into this ancient world which creates the nexus[26] whereby modern and ancient lives intersect and whereby our understanding is shaped and taken further.

This is made possible by a second aspect of understanding that informs and underpins Israel's interpretation as the source of authority. This relates to what Heschel described as 'constant study' or in the words of Kolitz, *learning*: 'Learning was thus supposed to introduce, as it indeed has, a new existential dimension in the life of a *learning* Jew, namely the *dimension of understanding as a mode of being in the world*.'[27]

In other words, learning is not regarded as an intellectual or academic apparatus whereby the text can be analysed, but indeed as being organically part of the human wrestling with the world of the text and the text of the world and the life which emanates from this reciprocal relationship.

Word and life

This leads to one of the central tenets of Judaism: The Torah is conceived as the Tree of life;[28] it is *life* instruction and in this sense it enables, shapes and facilitates our relationship with other people ... and thus with God. Therefore Emmanuel Levinas is correct when he suggests that the full spirit of the Torah is to be found in the assertion that the relationship with God is realised via the relationship with humans and that this coincides with social justice. The primary concern of the Torah is certainly an ethi-

---

25. The way Miskotte preferred to refer to the text of Scripture.
26. This is found, perhaps more than anything else, in the common questions, 'What do the people of the Bible and us have in common: the anxieties and joys of living; the sense of wonder and the resistance to it; the awareness of the hiding God and moments of longing to find a way to Him.' (*Between God and man*, 242).
27. Kolitz, *The Teacher*. vii. Heschel adds, 'It is not enough to accept or even to carry out the commandments. To study, to examine, to explore the Torah is a form of worship, a supreme duty.' (*Between God and man*, 247). Compare this to an attitude often found in Protestantism where study is not only eschewed, but regarded as the polar opposite of worship. Within this context, it can hardly be surprising that fundamentalism flourishes, because imitation becomes the only hermeneutical option.
28. Heschel, *Man is not alone*, 264.

cal one, but as such, its scope of interest is an all-encompassing one, dealing with the meaning of the world and life in general.[29]

Hence it can be concluded that the focus of the Jewish Scriptures according to Jewish understanding, is not God, but humankind. 'The bible does not deal with divinity but with humanity.'[30] This does not devalue the bible in any possible way; to the contrary, the human focus can only be properly understood within the context of the power of divine concern.

> it is as if God took these Hebrew words and breathed into them of His power, and the words became a live wire charged with His spirit. To this very day they are hyphens between heaven and earth.[31]

As the OT deals with public life, as well as the individual and the hidden life of the individual, it can hardly be called a 'spiritual' book in the way the word is mostly used in contemporary society. It doesn't deal with 'spiritual' matters as opposed to material, social or political issues and as such it doesn't lend itself easily to any Gnostic interpretation.

It is indeed this notion of being inseparably bound up with creation, with the world, the deeply existential character of the OT, which Miskotte reckoned as part of the 'plus' of the OT. In fact, without this 'naivety' of the OT, the exegesis and application of the NT is continually under threat of being reverted to 'spiritual' categories: in other words, universalistic and abstract interpretations.[32] There is certainly nothing neat[33] about the Hebrew bible and exactly therefore it reflects life as we experience it. It always leads us back to the realities of life, the realities of injustice, poverty and suffering. As Levinas has rightly observed, it leads us back to our own responsibilities.

> The fact that the relationship with the Divine crosses the relationship with men and coincides with social justice is therefore what epitomises the entire spirit of the Jewish Bible. Moses and the prophets preoccupied themselves not

---

29. NM Samuelson, *Jewish Philosophy. An historical introduction.* (London: Continuum, 2003), 38.
30. Heschel, *God in search of man*, 244.
31. Heschel, *God in search of man*, 244.
32. Miskotte, *Als de goden zwijgen*, 148.
33. T Cahill, *The gift of the Jews. How a Tribe of desert nomads changed the way everyone thinks and feels.* (New York: Doubleday, 1998), 246.

with the immortality of the soul but with the poor, the widow, the orphan and the stranger. The relationship with man in which contact with the Divine is established is not a kind of *spiritual friendship* but the sort that is manifested, tested and accomplished in a just economy and for which each man is fully responsible.[34]

This idea is of crucial importance and its significance stretches well beyond a mere call to social justice or worse, a call for public theology as opposed to a theology of personal salvation. It establishes a consistent unity of outward life and inner thought. Hence Judaism, as Heschel remarks,[35] never had a problem with the dichotomy of faith and works, an issue which has dominated Christianity for centuries after the Reformation.

Judaism's basic problem, 'What is right living?', also well and truly transcends any narrow understanding of teleological or utilitarian ethics. It is both a theological and an existential question which is contemplated against the hermeneutical horizon of Torah and tradition, of present needs and future implications. And again, the hermeneutical nexus is found in the *Deus praesens*, in the living God whose Word and presence invoke the questions and inspire the answers.

What this means and how it comes to its own, especially in a time of crisis, is demonstrated in the most profound way, in the life and thought of Dietrich Bonhoeffer.

By his own admission, it was in prison where Bonhoeffer really came to appreciate the OT by reinterpreting the NT in light of the 'Old' and by allowing himself to dwell on the OT questions, rather than jumping to NT answers prematurely. In a letter to Eberhard Bethge, dated Advent II, Bonhoeffer expresses the way he had come to perceive these things:

> My thoughts and feelings seem to be getting more and more like those of the Old Testament, and in recent months I have been reading the Old Testament much more than the New. It is only when one knows the unutterability of the name of God that one can utter the name of Jesus Christ; it only when one loves life and the earth so much that without them everything seems to be over that one may believe in the resurrection and a new world; it is only when one submits to God's

---

34. Levinas, *Difficult Freedom*, 19-20.
35. Heschel, *Between God and man*, 156.

law that one may speak of grace; and it is only when God's wrath and vengeance are hanging as grim realities over the heads of one's enemies that something of what it means to love and forgive them can touch our hearts. In my opinion it is not Christian to want to take our thoughts and feelings too quickly and too directly from the New Testament.[36]

What makes this quote particularly poignant is the manner in which the central tenets of Judaism as they are found in the OT are showing themselves in shaping Bonhoeffer's thought. However, the point here is not to show the extent of that influence,[37] but rather to call attention to the OT's role and influence in preparing Bonhoeffer for his witness at this crucial point in history, as well as the OT influence in his non-religious interpretation of the bible, one of the characteristics of his theology which made it such a powerful witness in post-modern times.

The real impact of the OT becomes particularly obvious towards Bonhoeffer's last months in prison—also the time when the most important part of his theological heritage was taking form. His wrestling with the idea of a non-religious worldly Christianity is very clearly (this is stated explicitly) done in the context of OT interpretation. As God is beyond in the midst of our lives, so the Church is in the middle of the village and therefore Christ is the Lord of the world. He adds, 'That is how it is in the OT, and in this sense we still read the NT far too little in the light of the Old.'[38]

This leads to the well-known assertion that Jesus calls men, not to a new religion, but to life.[39] In other words, following Christ is not something 'religious' or 'partial'; it involves the whole of one's life, where no distinction is made between the outward and the inward.[40]

This truly OT idea also opened Bonhoeffer's eyes to the flaws in regarding Christianity as a religion of redemption, or better formulated, a religion of *other*-worldly redemption. In the OT redemption is historical,

---

36. D Bonhoeffer, *Letters and Papers from prison*. (London: SCM Press, 1953), 38. Bonhoeffer also mentions that he had gone through the OT two and a half times and that he learnt a lot from it (24).
37. That has been done conclusively by, among others, Martin Kuske, *The Old Testament as the book of Christ. An appraisal of Bonhoeffer's interpretation*. (Philadelphia: Westminster Press, 1976).
38. Bonhoeffer, *Letters and Papers from prison*, 91-92.
39. Bonhoeffer, *Letters and Papers from prison*, 131.
40. Bonhoeffer, *Letters and Papers from prison*, 125.

that is, on this side of the grave: 'Israel is delivered out of Egypt so that it may live before God as God's people on earth.'[41]

Under the influence of the OT Bonhoeffer continues to flesh out his non-religious interpretation: 'Aren't righteousness and the Kingdom of God on earth the focus of everything? . . . It is not with the beyond that we are concerned, but with this world as created, preserved, subjected to laws, reconciled and restored.'[42] If we now ask: What is non-religious interpretation? The answer is: non-religious interpretation is neither metaphysical nor individual. Positively put, it is existential, worldly, and done within the contours of God's care for all of humanity. 'It follows that our relation to God is also a non-religious relationship, which is a worldly relationship or a "being there for others", in participation in the being of Jesus.'[43]

It was this, perhaps more than anything else, which made it possible for Bonhoeffer to understand that having faith in Jesus Christ doesn't mean to be willing to die devoutly for Him,[44] but rather to be willing to live completely in this world, even if that might mean not only bandaging the victims under the wheel, but to put a spoke in the wheel itself.[45]

Judaism and the renewal of Christianity (conclusion)

In a lecture titled 'The God of Israel and Christian renewal' Abraham Heschel commences with what is perhaps the crucial issue: 'Christian renewal should imply confrontation with Judaism out of which it emerged. Separated from its source, Christianity is easily exposed to principles alien to its spirit.'[46] Heschel's contribution is particularly significant because he takes us back to the importance of asking the right hermeneutical questions, the questions underpinning any understanding of the bible. He is correct in his assertion that the bible is easily respected as a source of dogma and not as a living history.

This is exactly the reason why Christianity has lost the memory of the questions preceding our reading of the bible. The Hebrew bible (and therefore by the same token, our OT) is not so much a book about God,

---

41. Bonhoeffer, *Letters and Papers from prison*, 119.
42. Bonhoeffer, *Letters and Papers from prison*, 92.
43. Bonhoeffer, *Letters and Papers from prison*, 139.
44. R Wind, *Dietrich Bonhoeffer: A Spoke in the wheel.* (Grand Rapids: Eerdmans, 1991), 16.
45. Wind, *Dietrich Bonhoeffe*, 69.
46. AJ Heschel, *Moral Grandeur and Spiritual audacity. Essays edited by Susannah Heschel* (New York: Farrar, Straus & Giroux, 1996), 272.

but a book about people. God's concern is not God, but God's concern is humankind.[47] Therefore we need to remember: the question, to which the bible is an answer, is not: Who is God? But indeed: What does God require of us?[48] It is almost impossible to even approach the issues of the authority of the bible, without this knowledge.

It is in recovering these questions that we realise how strong a bulwark the OT is against the problems the Church has had with both fundamentalism and secularism. As I have indicated in this paper, fundamentalism is almost no option in an understanding where the bible is appreciated, respected and accepted as the book of God *and* man.

Secondly, the bible as living history, as it was clearly appreciated by Dietrich Bonhoeffer, can help the Church realise that there is not preoccupation with the 'religious' in the bible; what counts is the secular.[49] In this sense, the bible (OT in particular) protects the Church against a spirituality which has lost touch with the real issues of society.

In the final instance, it is true that the reappropriation of OT is no panacea for the problems of the world; it is very much the point from where the Church can learn what the real problems are and how to take these problems seriously.

---

47. Heschel, *Moral Grandeur*, 276.
48. Heschel, *Moral Grandeur*, 274.
49. Heschel, *Moral Grandeur*, 277.

Chapter Seven
Approaching the New Testament as Source of Faith and Witness to Faith

William Loader

Hermeneutics is about more than homosexuality. But for many members of the Christian community the issue of biblical interpretation is defined in recent experience by such issues as whether to ordain people in an active homosexual relationship and, just slightly less recently, whether to ordain women as bishops or women at all. The list could be extended with the ever present caveat that such issues of dispute have a way of making themselves more central than they should be, creating not only problems of hermeneutics but also crises of identity. This is nothing new. Arguably early Christians' disputes over circumcision redefined the heart of Judaism for some then and since into unrecognisability.[1]

I want to approach the theme, *The Task of Theology Today, Hermeneutics and the Authority of Scripture* by looking at *yesterday*, more particular-

---

1. The classic work challenging such preconceptions which played themselves out across the Protestant- Catholic divide and in implicit antisemitism was that of Ed P Sanders, *Paul and Palestinian Judaism*, (London: SCM, 1977), which then gave rise in various forms to the so-called 'new perspective' on Paul. See the most recent discussions in James D G Dunn, *The New Perspective on Paul*, (Grand Rapids: Eerdmans, 2nd Edition, 2007); N Thomas Wright, *Paul in Fresh Perspective*, (Minneapolis: Fortress, 2006); Stephen G Westerholm, *Perspectives Old and New on Paul: The 'Lutheran Paul' and His Critics*, (Grand Rapids: Eerdmans, 2003); Frances Watson, *Paul, Judaism, and the Gentiles: Beyond the New Perspective*, (Grand Rapids: Eerdmans, 2007); Douglas A Campbell, *The Deliverance of God: An Apocalyptic Rereading of Justification in Paul* (Grand Rapids: Eerdmans, 2009). Allied to this was also a reassessment of attitudes towards the Torah in Judaism, which, in turn, brought more differentiated treatments of Jesus and the gospel tradition. On this see again the pioneering work of Ed P Sanders, *Jesus and Judaism*, (London: SCM, 1985). See also Philip Sigal, *The Halakhah of Jesus of Nazareth according to the Gospel of Matthew*, (Lanham MD, University of America Press, 1986; Atlanta: SBL, 2007); William Loader, *Jesus' Attitude towards the Law: A Study of the Gospels*, (Grand Rapids: Eerdmans, 2002).

ly, by considering issues over hermeneutics back in New Testament times inasmuch as these can be gleaned with some degree of probability from its writings. I do so, nevertheless, as a task of theology *today*, hence my title, which speaks of 'the New Testament as a Source of Faith and Witness to Faith' because I am aware that such differences have sometimes been other than a celebration of diversity and instead been a site of pain and disease within the body. I do so as a white middle class reasonably well off western heterosexual male who therefore needs conversation with others.

Hermeneutics in Mark: Looking at Mark 7:1–23

Let me begin with Mark's retelling of the encounter between Jesus and some Pharisees who had come down from Jerusalem and were complaining that his disciples had eaten bread with unwashed hands (7:1–23).[2] In a bald generalisation, which should not be statistically pressed, Mark explains that 'all Jews' practice such lustrations, including immersing themselves after returning from the market, and ritually washing cups, pots, kettles, and possibly beds (7:3–4).[3] Mark's locality may be the diaspora, but the narrative's locality, Galilee, coheres well with what we otherwise know of the scene, where holiness movements apparently had sufficiently broad influence to leave traces in archaeology of immersion pools and stone jars for purification.[4] Mark identifies such strictures as the tradition of the elders (7:5). If the description of the practices itself does not already indicate some disparagement,[5] the subsequent engagement is certainly confronting. It shows Jesus using Isa 29:13 to expose the disparity between such strictures and attitudes of the heart (7:6–8) and in the same vein, and perhaps consequentially, identifies that such disparity leads also to injustice, as in the misuse of corban (7:9–13).

---

2. For what follows see Loader, *Jesus' Attitude*, 71–79; and William Loader, 'Mark 7:1–23 and the Historical Jesus', *Colloquium* 30/2 (1998): 123–51.
3. There is a textual variant that adds beds to the list. Some argue its authenticity: see James G Crossley, 'Halakah and Mark 7.4: "...and beds"' in *Journal for the Study of the New Testament* 25 (2003): 433–47.
4. On this see Jonathan L Reed, *Archaeology and the Galilean Jesus: A re-examination of the Evidence* (Harrisburg, PA: Trinity, 2002), 43–52. See also Sean Freyne, 'Archaeology and the Historical Jesus', in *Jesus and Archaeology*, edited by James H Charlesworth (Grand Rapids: Eerdmans, 2006), 64–83.
5. So Heikki Sariola, *Markus und das Gesetz: Eine redaktionsgeschichtliche Untersuchung* (Annales Academiae Scientiarum Fennicae Dissertationes Humanarum Litterarum 56), (Helsinki: Suomalainen Tiedeakatemia, 1990), 51; Loader, *Jesus' Attitude*, 78.

The challenge reaches it climax, marked by a special summoning of the hearers, in the declaration that nothing entering a person from outside can make them unclean, but only what comes from within (7:14-15). It effectively dismisses the presuppositions upon which the complaint and the various practices are based. Not only do such things not have this effect; they are also not able to have this effect. This is stating the obvious and perhaps with literal pungency, if what the disciples then call a parable can be reduced to: what stinks is not what enters but what comes out.[6]

It is not stating the obvious in all settings, including, apparently for the disciples, who seek further clarification of 'the parable' (7:17) in a sequence of public statement and private elaboration typical of Mark's anecdotes and perhaps reflecting prior didactic use of the stories (compare 4:10; 9:28; 10:10). As elsewhere in Mark, the disciples are shown as not seeing the obvious (7:18a; compare 8:17–21), before the explanation follows which now returns the focus to food, the stomach and the toilet (7:18b–19). The climax declares that real impurity is what comes from the heart or mind: attitudes that produce immoral and unethical behaviour, matching the emphasis of the antitheses of the Sermon on the Mount (7:20–23; compare Matt 5:21–48).

In the midst of this explanation Mark seemingly appends a parenthesis: καθαρίζων πάντα τὰ βρώματα (7:19b), which means literally: 'cleansing all foods'. Some manuscripts read καθαρίζον, a neuter participle, which would then be describing what happens when food goes through us and into the toilet.[7] The far better attested reading refers to what Jesus was doing.[8] In the broader context of Mark it is a typical reference to Jesus' authority (compare 2:10, 17a, 28). As elsewhere, in the immediate context we see that it is more than an authoritative assertion (compare 2:9, 17b, 25–27). It summarises the import of an argument. This scarcely means that Jesus was literally at that point cleansing foods or that Jesus was initiating a change of rules, understood within a theology of dis-

---

6. For literal concern with human waste see 1QM/1Q33 7.6-7 and 11QT^a/11Q19 46.13-16 and see Bruce J Malina, 'A Conflict Approach to Mark 7', *Forum* 4 (1988): 3-30 especially 23.
7. So Malina, 'Mark 7', 22-25; Similarly Richard A Horsley, *Hearing the Whole Story: The Politics of Plot in Mark's Gospel* (Louisville, KY: Westminster John Knox, 2001), 171.
8. So Robert Banks, *Jesus and the Law in the Synoptic Tradition* (Society for New Testament Studies Monograph Series 28) (Cambridge: Cambridge University Press, 1975), 144; Richard T France, *The Gospel of Mark: A Commentary on the Greek Text*, (Grand Rapids, MI: Eerdmans; Carlisle: Paternoster, 2002), 276.

pensation, the new replacing the old.⁹ That is not how the context argues. It is not giving reasons why what was once valid is now being set aside. It is not about timing, but about substance. Jesus showed that all foods are clean, that no foods are unclean. Why? Because, by implication, it should be 'obvious': foods cannot make people unclean since they simply enter the stomach and then go out into the toilet. Thus, it is being argued, by their very nature they cannot make people unclean and never could have. It is an appeal to common sense.¹⁰

Mark's hearers might have seen the implications as relating to a range of issues. The immediate context assumes some kind of contamination of foods from unwashed hands and other unclean items. The saying, which speaks of nothing external, suggests the range of broader concerns with impurity, including food. For some, the issue of clean and unclean animals may have sprung to mind (Leviticus 11) or meat bought at the market which more than likely derived from pagan temples. In the broader context of the concerns of Mark 6-8, where food features as a common motif and the focus is on Jews and non-Jews, dealing with issues of external purity especially in relation to foods was highly relevant. It removed potential barriers between Jews and non-Jews. Mark and his predecessors were probably aware of the problems that such barriers caused. We are fortunate to have Paul's account of the division over common meals at Antioch (Gal 2:11–14). As it stands Mark's narrative employs the feeding of the 5000, replete with symbolism of Israel, and the feeding of 4000 non-Jews in non-Jewish land as a celebration of the food of the gospel reaching both.¹¹

When, at its conclusion, Mark has Jesus test the disciples' perception of the obvious again, having recalled the numbers of baskets of left-overs—12 and 7—they fail (8:14–21), but Mark's hearers surely do see and appreciate the irony of Mark's sequel to that episode which reports Jesus healing a

---

9. Compare M Eugene Boring, *Mark: A Commentary* (Louisville, KY: Westminster John Knox, 2006), 203; Ben Witherington, *The Gospel of Mark: A Socio-Rhetorical Commentary* (Grand Rapids MI: Eerdmans, 2001), 228–31; France, *Mark*, 289–91; J Marcus, *Mark 1-8* (Anchor Bible Commentary 27) (New York: Doubleday, 2000), 453–54.
10. So rightly Sariola, *Markus*, 255–61.
11. See Loader, *Jesus' Attitude*, 84–85; U Luz, in R Smend and U Luz, *Gesetz* (Kohlhammer Taschenbücher—Biblische Konfrontationen 1015) (Stuttgart: Kohlhammer, 1981), 58-156 at 118; Sariola, *Markus*, 62-3. On the symbolism see Boring, *Mark*, 218-9; Francis J Moloney, *The Gospel of Mark: A Commentary*, (Peabody, MA: Hendrickson, 2002), 155; Marcus, *Mark*, who declares that Mark 'seems to belong to the number-obsessed camp' (508), though earlier denying it (489–90, 497).

man who was blind and dumb (8:22-26). Mark had done something similar earlier when he immediately followed our anecdote about clean and unclean with the risqué account of Jesus' meeting with a Syro-Phoenician woman, a non-Jew, his voicing the traditional demarcation, and then his crossing the boundary in responding to her cry (7:24-30).[12] Mark's narrative celebrates what Ephesians describes as the breaking down of the barrier between Jew and Gentile: 'For he is our peace, who in his flesh has made both one and broken down the dividing wall, the enmity, having abolished the law with its commandments and ordinances, that he might create in himself one new humanity in place of the two, thus making peace' (2:14-15).

This sounds all very straightforward, but it is far from being so. The quotation from Ephesians might alert us to the fact that we are dealing here with more than just Jewish scruples. We are dealing with scripture. That is certainly the implication in Mark. In Mark's depiction Jesus is declaring clean what the scriptures declare unclean and doing so because the notion that external foods can make a person unclean simply 'doesn't make sense'. A combination of rational argument, reflecting popular critique of religious scruples, and Jesus' authority warrants calling into question biblical law about external impurity. But biblical law about purity and impurity related to externals is extensive and foundational to the temple cult and also much else. Space forbids me here to show how this coheres with Mark's approach elsewhere.[13] For him the temple is really only a place of prayer. Gentile land is not unclean.[14] It is important to be clear: Mark is not saying that Jesus declares that these laws were once valid and have now been superseded, but rather that they never were valid in the first place, as allegedly something which should be 'obvious'.

---

12. See William Loader, 'Challenged at the Boundaries: A Conservative Jesus in Mark's Tradition', in the *Journal for the Study of the New Testament* 63 (1996): 45-61, especially at 45-51.
13. See the discussion in Loader, *Jesus' Attitude*, 122-36; William Loader, *Jesus and the Fundamentalism of his Day* (Grand Rapids: Eerdmans, 2001), 31-52.
14. The two anecdotes in Mark 5, the encounters with the Gerasene demoniac in Gentile territory and with the two women in Jewish territory, now celebrate in Mark the good news to Gentiles and Jews, like the feedings of the 4000 and 5000, but they began as stories which depended for their potency on Jewish assumptions about impurity that Mark no longer espouses. On this see Loader, *Jesus' Attitude*, 58-64.

Hermeneutics in Matthew: Looking at Matthew 15:1–20

An approach that combined popular rational argument about the 'obvious' and Jesus' authority to set aside large sections of scripture was just as much likely to evoke controversy then as it does now. The refrains, 'The Bible is the Word of God: how can you set aside Scripture? You are watering down Scripture to placate people', have a long history, reaching far back into the early days of the church. Not everyone then or now would want to go along with Mark.

Matthew didn't, but Matthew loved Mark's portrait of Jesus otherwise, making it, as I still assume as the most viable explanation, the grid for his own expanded presentation. On the one hand, his own orientation, perhaps reflecting a predominantly Jewish setting where Christian Jews had sought unsuccessfully to establish a Jesus scribal tradition as the norm for the synagogue, did not sit comfortably with the idea that anything should be set aside. On the other hand, he also employed traditions, commonly identified as Q, which plainly declared that not a stroke of the law was to fall and that any who taught as much—as some obviously did—would be called least in the kingdom (5:17–19).[15] Matthew is not drawing on these traditions only to trump them with the claim that on the contrary, now that Jesus has come, they are to be set aside.[16] Such views have rested on assumptions which read variation in interpreting Torah as evidence of

---

15. So R Mohrlang, *Matthew and Paul: A Comparison of Ethical Perspectives* (Society for New Testament Studies Monograph Series, 48) (Cambridge: Cambridge University Press, 1984), 14–5, 22–6; Dale C Allison, *The New Moses: A Matthean Typology*, (Minneapolis MN: Fortress, 1993), 185–90, 320–3; KR Snodgrass, 'Matthew and the Law', in *Treasures Old and New: Contributions to Matthean Studies*, edited by DR Bauer and MA Powell, (Society of Biblical Literature Symposium Series 1, (Atlanta, GA: Scholars, 1996), 99–127, 111–118; John H Nolland, *The Gospel of Matthew: A Commentary on the Greek Text* (New International Greek Testament Commentary) (Grand Rapids, MI: Eerdmans; Bletchey: Paternoster, 2005), 218–24.
16. Compare Banks, *Law*, 217–8; John P Meier, *Law and History in Matthew's Gospel: A Redactional Study of Mt 5:17–48*, Analecta Biblica 71, (Rome: Pontifical Biblical Institute, 1976), 30, 59–65; 89, 168; RT France, *The Gospel of Matthew* (New International Greek Testament Commentary) (Grand Rapids, MI: Eerdmans, 2007), 187–8; Roland Deines, *Die Gerechtigkeit der Tora im Reich des Messias: Mt 5,13–20 als Schlüsseltext der matthäischen Theologie* (Wissenschaftliche Untersuchungen zum Neuen Testament, 177), (Tübingen: Mohr Siebeck, 2004); Paul Foster, *Community, Law and Mission in Matthew's Gospel* (Wissenschaftliche Untersuchungen zum Neuen Testament, 2.177) (Tübingen: Mohr Siebeck, 2004), who argues that, read in the light of 5:21–48, which he sees differentiating Jesus and Moses and rescinding some laws, 5:17–20 cannot intend upholding of the Law (94–5; 121–2, 141, 147, 211).

setting it aside in a way that recent research has rightly called into question, since even the most devout adherents of Torah saw no problems in enhancing strictness of some laws and modifying others, even rewriting them to address new situations, as evident for instance in the Temple Scroll.[17] Matthew's and Q's perspective is well represented in the saying about tithes: 'Woe to you, scribes and Pharisees, hypocrites! For you tithe mint, dill, and cummin, and have neglected the weightier matters of the law: justice and mercy and faith. It is these you ought to have practiced without neglecting the others' (23:23; Luke 11:42). In Matthew's hermeneutical stance nothing is set aside, not even tithing herbs, which takes biblical law to the extreme, but priorities are set and, if need be, some may override others.

Accordingly, Matthew's version of the encounter between Jesus and the critics over his disciples' eating with unwashed hands (15:1–20) deletes Mark's global explanation at the beginning (Mark 7:2-4), deletes Mark's summary of the import of the conversation (Mark 7:18b), and in the wider context unravels Mark's celebration of Jews and Gentiles receiving the food of the gospel: the 4000 now seem to be Jews in Jewish land, and Jesus no longer asks the disciples about the number of baskets, but focuses instead on the impact of the miracles (16:5–12).[18] Matthew has the controversy now end with the conclusion that there is no need to eat with unwashed hands (15:20). The effect is to produce a reading of the story according to which it remains a dispute about Jewish scruples and is not about biblical law and so does not set it aside.

Thus, while Matthew still had a version of the saying about food entering the body and retains the explanations which depict its destiny (15:11), the contrast is now not an absolute one,[19] but a relative one.[20] It might

---

17. On this see Sigal, *The Halakah of Jesus of Nazareth*, 154–9; Karlheinz Müller, 'Forschungsgeschichtliche Anmerkungen zum Thema "Jesus von Nazareth und das Gesetz": Versuch einer Zwischenbilanz', in *Kirche und Volk Gottes: FS für Jürgen Roloff*, edited by Martin Karrer, (Neukirchen-Vluyn: Neukirchener Verlag, 2000), 58–77; Snodgrass, 'Matthew', 118-9; Warren Carter, 'Matthew's Gospel: Jewish Christianity, Christian Judaism, or Neither?' in *Jewish Christianity Reconsidered*, edited by M Jackson-McCabe, (Minneapolis MN: Fortress, 2007), 155–79, 166–7.
18. For the following see Loader, *Jesus' Attitude*, 210–20.
19. Compare France, *Mark*, 278–9; France, *Matthew*, 180.
20. So Ulrich Luz, *Das Evangelium nach Matthäus (Mt 8–17)* (Evangelisch-Katholische Kommentare, ½) (Zürich: Benziger; Neukirchen-Vluyn: Neukirchener Verlag, 1990), 424–5, 428; Nolland, *Matthew*, 620; James DG Dunn, *Jesus Remembered* (Christianity in the Making, Volume 1) (Grand Rapids MI: Eerdmans, 2003), 576; T Kazen, *Jesus and Purity Halakhah: Was Jesus Indifferent to Impurity?* (Coniectanea Biblica 38)

be paraphrased: not so much what enters a person's mouth makes them unclean as what comes out of it. You still attend to biblical laws about clean and unclean just as you do to tithing (23:23), but you need to see where the priority lies. The contrast matches Hosea 6:6, 'I desire mercy not sacrifice', understood not as meaning: I do not want sacrifice, but as: I desire mercy and compassion more than sacrifice, a common theme and common meaning of such contrasts in Jewish tradition, introduced twice by Matthew in retelling Mark's controversy stories (9:13; 12:7). Matthew's hermeneutical move—or if you favour Matthew's independence, Matthew's distinctive stance—represents a model which affirms scripture without exception but differentiates within it. The focus is attitude rather than merely behaviours (5:21–48) and that attitude is characterised by compassion and righteousness (meaning something close to compassion in Matthew). It is on not imposing unduly heavy burdens in applying scripture to life and bearing the yoke (compare 11:28–30; 23:2–4). Thus, according to Matthew, in a nice twist of Mark's saying, Jesus taught with authority and not as *their* scribes (7:29; compare Mark 1:22). Jesus is the scribe *par excellence* (cf 13:52).

Hermeneutics in Luke: The Great Omission

It is perhaps not surprising that Luke, who, I assume, also inherits Q, must have also encountered Mark 7 with hesitation. In Acts, his Paul is Torah-observant to the end despite rumours asserting the opposite (Acts 20:20–22).[21] Luke's comment that the Law and the Prophets were under assault and now the same is happening to the kingdom of God (Luke 16:16) does not in my view dismiss the former as ceasing to be in force, as some have thought.[22] Rather it finds its explanation in his version of the saying about

---

(Stockholm: Almqvist & Wiksell, 2002), 86; Marcus, *Mark*, 453; Adela Y Collins, *Mark: A Commentary* (Hermeneia) (Minneapolis MN: Fortress, 2007), 354, who speaks of Mark's explanatory comment as 'a giant step further' (356).

21. Jacob Jervell, 'The Law in Luke–Acts', in Jacob Jervell, *Luke and the People of God: A New Look at Luke–Acts*, (Minneapolis MN: Augsburg, 1972), 133–52, 140–41; Jacob Jervell, *Die Apostelgeschichte*, (Kritisch-Exegetische Kommentare, 3) (Göttingen: Vandenhoeck & Ruprecht, 1998), 525–6; Charles Kingsley Barrett, *A Critical and Exegetical Commentary on the Acts of the Apostles: Volume II*, (International Critical Commentary) (Edinburgh: T&T Clark, 1998), 1013.

22. Craig L Blomberg, 'The Law in Luke–Acts', in the *Journal for the Study of the New Testament* 22 (1984): 53–80 at 61; similarly Darrell Bock, *Luke 1:1 – 9:50*, (Grand Rapids, MI: Baker, 1994), 39–40. Hans Conzelmann, *The Theology of Saint Luke* (Lon-

the Law's sanctity losing not a stroke of its validity (16:17), and a severe exposition of the divorce law to reinforce the point (16:18).[23] His setting seems other than Matthew's and he is probably writing as a Gentile in a predominantly Gentile context but also with a keen awareness of Jewish Christianity and mixed groups. Issues of continuity both ways, with Israel and with his church, and unity are paramount. What does Luke do with Mark 7 and its context?

Either he had a copy in which these sections were happily lost or, more likely, he chose to omit them.[24] The silent treatment does not last because in Acts he revisits the issues. He cannot help but acknowledge that some elements of scripture's abiding demands were set aside—notably circumcision—but portrays these as exceptions warranted by divine intervention for a significantly changed situation, effectively exceptions which proved the rule, namely that the rest of Torah remained in force.[25] The Apostolic Decree has Gentiles also observe what in Torah applies to them (Leviticus 17–18).[26] Luke depicts the early Christians' links with the temple as very positive and accusations to the contrary as quite wrong (Acts 3:1; 5:12, 25; 6:13). Peter's vision sounds like the setting aside of food laws, at least pertaining to clean and unclean animals, and perhaps it did mean that in earlier retellings (Acts 10:9–16). In Luke's retelling the point appears, however, not to be food at all but people: no person is unclean; therefore it is acceptable to enter Gentile homes and eat with them (10:17, 28,

---

don: Faber and Faber, 1960), first published as *Die Mitte der Zeit*, (Tübingen: Mohr Siebeck, 1953, 2nd edition, 1957), argued that they remained in force during the period up to the Jerusalem Council, but after that lost their force according to Luke (23, 147, 159-61); similarly Hans Hübner, *Das Gesetz in der synoptischen Tradition*, (Göttingen: Vandenhoeck & Ruprecht, 2nd edition, 1986), 208, who notes Torah observance in the infancy narratives and as explaining Luke's omission of Mark 10:2-9 (207-8); K Salo, *Luke's Treatment of the Law: A Redaction-Critical Investigation* (Annales Academiae Scientiarum Fennicae Dissertationes Humanarum Litterarum, 57) (Helsinki: Suomalainen Tiedeakatemia, 1991), 31-2.

23. Jervell, 'Law', 133-52; Similarly Joseph A Fitzmyer, 'The Jewish People and the Mosaic Law in Luke-Acts', in Joseph A Fitzmyer, *Luke the Theologian: Aspects of his Teaching* (London: Chapman, 1989), 175-202; Hans Klein, *Das Lukasevangelium*, Kritisch-Exegetische Kommentare, (Göttingen: Vandenhoeck & Ruprecht, 2006), 549.
24. Loader, *Jesus' Attitude*, 320-1.
25. Jervell, *Apostelgeschichte*, 318; Loader, *Jesus' Attitude*, 368-71.
26. Jervell, 'Law', 144; Fitzmyer, 'Jewish People', 202 n. 45; compare also M Klinghardt, *Gesetz und Volk Gottes: Das lukanische Verständnis des Gesetzes* (Wissenschaftliche Untersuchungen zum Neuen Testament, 32) (Tübingen: Mohr Siebeck, 1988), 186-200, 205-66, 217.

34; compare Luke 7:1–10).²⁷ Unfortunately, the extent of Luke's meaning, whether he affirms Mark's point or avoids it, is, to me, at this stage unclear. I am inclined on balance to align Luke with Matthew's hermeneutics. The alternative is to posit a degree of inconsistency in Luke-Acts,²⁸ which I think less likely.

Hermeneutics Behind the Gospels: Looking to Jesus

I find what the Q tradition preserves of Jesus' stance towards the Law to be coherent with what I find elsewhere in widely recognised early Jesus material. In other words, if the anecdote which has come into Mark 7 has its origins in an encounter during Jesus' ministry, as, I think, is the case with many of his anecdotes, even if in a less elaborated form, then its chief saying on the lips of Jesus would have meant: not so much what enters a person makes them unclean as what exits them,²⁹ reflecting the rhetorical pattern of inclusive antitheses used in the tradition.³⁰ It has the twofold

---

27. On this see PJ Tomson, 'Jewish purity laws as viewed by the Church fathers and by the early followers of Jesus', in *Purity and holiness: The Heritage of Leviticus*, edited by MJHM Poorthuis and J Schwartz (Leiden: Brill, 2000), 73–91 at 83–4, 89.
28. Stephen G Wilson, *Luke and the Law* (Society for New Testament Studies Monograph Series, 50) (Cambridge: Cambridge University Press, 1983), 57, who explains the absence of Mark 7:1–23 as missing in Luke's source and omission of 10:2–12 for lack of interest (52–5); see also K Syreeni, 'Matthew, Luke, and the Law: A Study in Hermeneutical Exegesis', in *The Law in the Bible and its Environment*, edited by T Veijola (Finnish Exegetical Studies 51) (Helsinki: Finnish Exegetical Society; Göttingen: Vandenhoeck & Ruprecht, 1990), 126–57 at 145–6.
29. So Tom Holmén, *Jesus and Jewish Covenant Thinking* (Biblical Interpretation Series, 55) (Leiden: Brill, 2001), 237–46; Dunn, *Jesus Remembered*, 576; Kazen, *Jesus*, 86, 88; SM Bryan, *Jesus and Israel's Traditions of Judgement and Restoration* (Society for New Testament Studies Monograph Series, 117) (Cambridge: Cambridge University Press, 2002), 167. Compare Jürgen Becker, *Jesus von Nazaret* (Berlin: de Gruyter, 1995), 381–7; and, as typical of the so-called second quest for the historical Jesus which interpreted it as abrogation: Ernst Käsemann, 'The Problem of the Historical Jesus', in Ernst Käsemann, *Essays on New Testament Themes* (Studies in Biblical Theology, 41) (London: SCM, 1964), 15–47 at 39.
30. For further examples of inclusive contrasts formulated absolutely see Ps 40:6; 51:16–17; *Aristeas* 234; Mark 9:37; 13:11, and Ed P Sanders, *Jewish Law from Jesus to the Mishnah*, (London: SCM; Philadelphia, PA: Trinity, 1990), 28; Roger P Booth, *Jesus and the Laws of Purity: Tradition History and Legal History in Mark 7* (Journal for the Study of the New Testament Supplement Series, 13) (Sheffield: JSOT Press, 1986), 69–71. WD Davies, and DC Allison, *A Critical and Exegetical Commentary on the Gospel according to Saint Matthew, Vol II: VIII-XVIII* (International Critical Commentary) (Edinburgh, T&T Clark, 1991), point to a similar structure of thought in Matthew's

playful structure characteristic of so many such sayings attributed to Jesus (Mark 2:9; 2:17a; 2:27; 3:4; 10:9; 12:17; 12:27), and like many of them probably intended the humour which some will have sniffed.

Beside the argument from coherence within the early sayings attributed to Jesus, there is also an argument from coherence within his and subsequent history. Had Jesus advocated setting scripture aside absolutely in this way, with or without the supplementary arguments, which may be secondary, that would have been extremely unusual within the diverse Judaism of the time and highly offensive, such that one would have expected it among charges levelled against him, not least in his trial.[31] Despite arguments to the contrary, it is also hard to understand the heat of such controversy in the early church among believers, including Peter and James, had Jesus ruled so clearly on such matters.[32]

Without being able to rehearse what requires an examination of a wide range of evidence, I conclude in summary in relation to Jesus that he was Torah-observant, and that controversies in his ministry arose over interpretation, including under what circumstances one priority might override another. In that sense the tradition of Matthew and Luke (and Q) accurately depict a hermeneutical stance which was affirming scripture, but differentiated within it,[33] and understood the saying about food inclusively. The impression one has from Mark and Mark's anecdotes, which may also be accurate, is that issues of conflict over Law arose mainly incidentally, while Jesus was doing something else. Jesus' announcement of God's coming reign and his claim already to some extent to bring its reality into his world through his exorcisms, healing, and engagement with people, were his focal point, not interpretation of biblical law. He stood in a prophetic and wisdom tradition which will have shaped both what he said about hope and its present reality and what he said when chal-

---

antitheses (527-31).
31. So JR Donahue and DJ Harrington, *The Gospel of Mark* (Sacra Pagina, 2) (Collegeville, MN: Liturgical, 2002), 228.
32. See Dunn, *Jesus Remembered*, 574-6; Sanders, *Jewish Law*, 28; Booth, *Purity*, 206, 219; Luz, *Matthäus* 2, 424.
33. Similarly Marcus, *Mark*, 453; Luz, *Matthäus* 2, 424; Davies and Allison, *Matthew* 2, 528-31; Nolland, *Matthew*, 621; Dunn, *Jesus Remembered*, 574-6. Compare Heikki Räisänen, 'Jesus and the Food Laws: Reflections on Mark 7:15', in Heikki Räisänen *Jesus, Paul and Torah* (Journal for the Study of the New Testament Supplement Series, 43) (Sheffield: JSOT Press, 1992), 127-48, who suggests that Christians, breaking with the dietary code in contexts of Gentile conversion in Palestine, created the saying (139-48).

lenged about his behaviour. His cryptic quips, which represent that tradition, were, like his parables, universal enough to evoke parallels, indeed, until quite recently, for some to allege Cynic links now discredited,[34] and to enable people then and now to find a hermeneutical core set of values with which to face new situations.

Hermeneutics and Solid Systems: Confronting the Other

The stance of Jesus (and Matthew, Luke, and Q) had a long history in Hebrew thought, including not only its prophetic and wisdom but also its legal heritage. It was and is good Judaism. Circumcise your hearts not just your genitals is a strong tradition (Deut 10:16; 30:6; Jer 4:4). For some, however, this was problematic. We may recognise this if we consider the question about the greatest commandment and what comes second (compare Mark 12:29-30). A very natural reading of the commandment to love God is that you keep God's commandments. God's commandments are surely to be kept. It is not for us to differentiate among them, which amounts to our standing at a distance and imposing our value system on them and so on God. Some might describe this as fundamentalism, but, even if we tolerate the loose anachronism and recognise the similarities, we are probably identifying a more complex phenomenon. According to this way of thinking, there is an established system, a divine order. Some, indeed, reinforced it with their primitive science: as the heavenly bodies move in order, so God provides order for all of life (for example, 1 Enoch 1-5). Stoic notions of order would also lend support.

Such systems of thinking are complex and meet us in many forms. They may survive among many indigenous cultures where we notice that our distinctions between ethical and ritual or ceremonial law are not recognised. The harmony of these ordered worlds is sacrosanct. It remains intact. To violate it at any point is to violate the whole. Such systems often survive best in isolation without the relativising effects of colliding with other such systems.

It would be reductionist and inaccurate to suggest that Galilean Judaism was like this. This awareness may, however, enable us to enter more empathetically into its world and into our own where such phenomena occur. It is also doubtful that there are any purely closed systems. Nevertheless, one could see that any fracturing of the system would create crises

---

34. See the critical assessment of alleged Cynic links in Dunn, *Jesus Remembered*, 292–302.

of identity and accompanying anxiety, fear or rage. Within the Judaism of the time of Jesus we have diverse phenomena. We may assume that for many the differentiation between ethical and ritual or ceremonial law would not have been meaningful. Some holiness movements appear to have sought to bring greater refinement to the system in the name of keeping God's order. Our controversy about washing hands reflects these developments in Galilee. In a diasporan environment such thinking would operate in a strongly defensive mode, especially where Jewish identity was under threat. It is, to my mind, a mistake to focus only on a few identity markers, like circumcision, sabbath, and food. Something much larger was at stake and it expressed itself above all as commitment to Torah observance.

Yet alongside this response were others that embodied very different perspectives. At the simplest level, seeing that other systems exist beside my own and are espoused just as firmly as I espouse mine, can send me into defensive retreat. Or it can make me ask questions. We still see the benefits of people's exposure to other cultures today. One of the main effects can be to begin to differentiate within my tradition, between what I see as perhaps just our way of doing things and what I see as of fundamental value.[35] The latter may represent common values I find in other cultures, but need not. These processes appear to have been of major importance in shaping the religious world in major world cultures from China to India, Israel to Greece, especially from the sixth century BCE on.[36] The hierarchies of value celebrated in the prophets stem in part from such encounters. They help us make sense of seemingly irreverent questions like: what is the greatest commandment?

Jesus stands within such emerging traditions, probably as a result of exposure to turbulence and hope within his own Jewish traditions, rather than through contact with foreign cultures towards which his responses

---

35. We see this happening already in Luke who employs the word, 'customs', to describe Jewish biblical law (Acts 6:14; 21:21; 26:3; 28:17), setting them in one sense on a level with those of other nations, but still with the assumption that those of Israel were God-given. On this see Wilson, *Luke and the Law*, 1–11.
36. See Mircea Eliade, *A History of Religious Ideas: Volume 1: From the Stone Age to the Eleusinian Mysteries*, (London: Collins, 1978), for a brief account of these developments in each. On the impact of Jews' encounter with Greco-Roman Hellenism, producing diverse responses, see John J Collins, *Between Athens and Jerusalem: Jewish Identity in the Hellenistic diaspora* (Grand Rapids: Eerdmans, 2nd edition, 2000); Erich S Gruen, *Diaspora: Jews amidst Greeks and Roman* (Cambridge, MA: Harvard University Press, 2002).

are mostly rather conservative.[37] While I think there are signs that his vision included Gentiles (perhaps the birds in the parable of the mustard seed: Mark 4:30–32; Matt 13:31–32; Luke 13:18–19; compare Ezek 17:22–24), his primary focus was hope for his own people and engaging them now with the promise of the future and its forms of realisation in the present. This set his priorities, which inevitably clashed with those who took the total divine system approach or who espoused other priorities. His priorities, he claimed, directly and indirectly, were God's priorities. So the sabbath was made for people not people for the sabbath (Mark 2:27) and in most of his responses we see a theology at work, in the strictest sense, which portrayed God not as primarily concerned with the sanctity of the divine system of laws, but as concerned with bringing men and women back to a relationship with each other and with God which created a community of compassion and caring, a foretaste of future hope. While his images and sayings reflect biblical tradition, many of his responses in quip and parable stand more in the wisdom tradition of appealing to the obvious of human experience, including about human ingoings and outgoings. The theological common sense of the Prodigal Son and the Good Samaritan is like much in the wisdom tradition—universal.

Hermeneutics of Mark and Paul: The Case for Change

So where did Mark go wrong? Or did he? While some think Mark depends on Paul, I see only an indirect connection, if there is one at all.[38] I don't think Paul would have answered the rich man's inquiry about eternal life, for instance, by pointing to the commandments (compare Mark 10:17–22). He may have known a form of the saying which Mark preserves in 7:15.[39] His theology of the cross also differs significantly from Mark's. Paul, however, meets us from the early days of the movement when Christianity was confronted with a transposing of Jesus' hermeneutical issues into a new key in the light of a more acute problem. They had to face some issues that apparently Jesus never faced. Do we proclaim the good news of

---

37. See Loader, 'Challenged at the Boundaries'.
38. See Marcus, *Mark*, who sees Mark under Pauline influence but as 'not a member of a Pauline "school" in the same sense that the authors of Colossians-Ephesians and the Pastorals are; unlike them, he has not studied, internalised, and imitated Paul's letters' (75).
39. See the discussion in Holmén, *Jesus*, 248; Donahue and Harrington, *Mark*, 229; James DG Dunn, *Romans* (Word Biblical Commentary, 38B) (Dallas: Word, 1988), 819, 830.

the kingdom, and now Jesus' involvement in it as the Messiah, to Gentiles? Addressing Gentile sympathisers attending synagogues was unavoidable. But do we go to them directly? In any case, what do we do with them? The answer here was obvious because Israel had long experience in dealing with foreigners, especially when they joined their communities. You circumcise them and require them to observe all biblical laws pertaining to Gentiles (Gen 17:10–14).

That all should have been straightforward. But it wasn't. Both Luke's later account (Acts 15) and Paul's first hand account (Gal 2:1–10) enable us to see that when the early Christians gathered to find a solution, apparently a good decade and half into the movement, this was far from a peaceful symposium on hermeneutics. Those who held consistently to the biblical position mounted their missions, invaded places where Paul had been active and dogged him for the rest of his letter life (Gal 1:6–9; 3:1–5; Phil 3:2–4, 18–19). The others agreed to waive circumcision, leaving themselves open to the charge that this was a cheap ploy to win converts (Gal 1:9) and a betrayal of scripture and of God's people, Israel. The rationale appears to have been a combination of claiming divine guidance and seeing this as compassionate. In many places and times such argumentation has wobbled considerably. But even those who agreed on this could not agree on other matters. It is a wonder that the movement survived. Some took the stance that all of scripture's demands remained intact with only certain exceptions. Defining the exceptions was problematic. We can see at least a more conservative James, brother of Jesus, in itself an interesting reflection on the movement's starting point; Peter, who seems more open, but under pressure bows to James (see Gal 2:11–14); Paul, and, beyond him, some who seemed to have abandoned scripture altogether.[40]

We are so fortunate to have the letters of Paul, which enable us to see elements of his stance. The occasional nature of his correspondence is a blessing: we can see theology in practice; and a challenge: he sometimes appears to make conflicting statements which have generated diverse reconstructions of his stance, no less today than earlier.

My reading is that Paul saw himself standing firmly within the tradition of his people.[41] He was sensitive to the charge that he had abandoned

---

40. One of the standard works on diversity in early Christianity remains James DG Dunn, *Unity and Diversity in the New Testament: An Enquiry into the Character of Earliest Christianity* (London: SCM, 2nd edition, 1990).
41. See also Francis Watson, *Paul and the Hermeneutics of Faith*, (London: T&T Clark, 2004), who argues that Paul's stands within the range of Jewish interpretation as he

them and defended himself with passion and with a range of arguments culminating in the assertion of faith that all Israel would be saved, but that how was a mystery in God's hands (Rom 11:25-26). I think he sustains his stance consistently that Christians, Jews and Gentiles, are not under the Law, but defends that stance against the view that he is thereby doing away with the Law, that is, the scripture, a charge doubtless laid against him along with others that his stance encouraged lawlessness (compare Rom 3:1-8; 6:1). People could easily have cited Corinth as a case in point.

In Romans in particular, Paul claims that Christians uphold the law (3:31). They do so however as a result of walking in the Spirit, which produces love in them that more than fulfils the demands of the law (8:1-4), since it is, indeed, how one might summarise the law (13:8-10; Gal 5:13-15, 22-23). Paul can only do so by affirming some things but denying others. Thus he employs what in biblical and Jewish tradition were relative contrasts, about circumcision of the heart mattering more than literal circumcision, and true inward Judaism as opposed to outward Judaism, and turns them into absolute contrasts (Rom 2:25-29). With that, we begin to leave the outward Judaism behind. Jews (and many Christian Jews) would have seen this as a long way from upholding the Law. Paul argues in his own way from scripture to justify his case, partly to cite the example of Abraham, who became for him a model of faith without the law (Rom 4:1-22), and partly by arguing that God has initiated a change in covenant history, so that whereas the Law applied until Christ, after Christ it no longer does so (Rom 7:1-6; Gal 3:15-22).

This, we should note, is different from Mark's argumentation that external purity laws never made sense anyway (Mark 7:15). Paul's arguments are complex and at times he appears to come close to disparaging the external, but stops short. We find a similar tension in Hebrews, which also espouses a change in covenant history, but can nonetheless describe the old as useless with its external focus (7:18; 9:13-14). While the fourth gospel also has Jesus declare that the flesh does not profit (6:63) and deems the old order given through Moses to have been God's gift at the level of flesh only until Christ (1:17), it never disparages the old in itself.[42] It dis-

---

engages his tradition (27-29).

42. See the discussion in William Loader, 'Jesus and the Law in John', in *Theology and Christology in the Fourth Gospel: Essays by Members of the Johannine Writings Seminar*, edited by G van Belle, JG van der Watt and P Maritz (Bibliotheca Ephemeridum Theologicarum Lovaniensium, 184), (Leuven: Leuven University Press; Leuven: Peeters, 2005), 135-54.

parages those who continue with it and fail to see that its only role now is to be a body of witness to Christ.

So, back to Paul and Paul's hermeneutics: what accounts for the shift? Was it that his christology alone dictated it? But then others who proclaimed Christ saw no need to set scripture aside. I suspect that the issues are much wider than Paul and belong to some crucial theologising done when the new movement encountered Gentile followers. Unlike the toll collectors and sinners who were children of Abraham, these were Gentiles. I suspect nevertheless that the same priority given to compassion which overrode other concerns about impurity and immoral company during the ministry of Jesus, now overrode similar concerns about Gentiles. The key shift came when incidental overriding became permanent, effectively setting aside certain biblical commandments. In some ways the less defined laws about unholy company were much more problematic than circumcision, but arguably compassion motivated the change.

Beside this, other factors were doubtless at work, including a relativising of particularisms of the Jewish system: special days, special places, special foods. None of it would have happened without a christology which saw God in Christ and a theology that saw God as compassionate and reconciling which had firm roots in scripture. Once the move was made, secondary rationalisation and reflection promoted larger solutions and for Paul led to a radically new basis for ethics and for law now thoroughly christocentric. Driving it ultimately, as with Jesus, was not scribal tradition, but prophetic hope and a theology informed by the theology of Jesus.

Concluding Reflection

The New Testament collection embraces a diversity of approaches to scripture, but not a wild one. Informing both the relativising approach of Matthew, Luke, Q, and ultimately Jesus, and the adaptive and selective approach of Paul and Mark and related traditions is a theology of grace. Both stand in conflict with a tradition of intricate divine order based on a theology of sustaining a system, applied later to the New Testament or to the whole Bible. All three approaches live on today, in their own way. One might argue that if our collected New Testament writings can embrace the diversity between the first two, it can do so today, but both need to engage the dangers of the third approach, addressing its fears and opening alternative ways. The age old effects of exposure to other systems which creatively relativises one's own and sends one seeking what matters most and seeing the wood for the trees can still be realised—and needs to be, even more urgently today among the macro-systems of major religions and cultures.

As for the other two models of hermeneutics, both function best when, as with Jesus, their task becomes incidental to the larger vision of the breaking in of the kingdom, including its good news for the poor, compassion for all people, reconciliation of all with God and with one another in peace. For people have a way of finding in these scriptures a source for their faith and hope or missing it despite the best efforts of those seeking to employ hermeneutics to determine ethics. That vision, represented in the eucharistic feast and ultimately in the being of God, needs to be the starting point of every hermeneutical enterprise, to which we come as women, as men, as rich, as poor, as culturally diverse, as experientially distinct, seeking hope and peace. For me that means critical engagement with the witnesses of faith in the scriptures informed by what I seek to identify as its core and doing so in the confidence that these continue to bear life and hope in our world.

Chapter Eight
Dog-throttling:
Nineteenth Century dogmatic / cultural constructions of the Syrophoenician Woman

Alan H Cadwallader

Introduction

In 1966, Roy Harrisville considered that 'the history of nineteenth and twentieth-century theology could well be written by the light of our text'.[1] The text was Mark 7:24–30, the story of the Syrophoenician woman. Indeed, nineteenth century lines have determined subsequent interpretation, whether as the code to embellish or the taboo from which to break.

Pre-eminent in that interpretation were the nature and meaning of the 'word'. That 'word' was predominantly the philosophical construction of the Idea(l), understood in christian terms to be the divine Son of God. The key debate centred on the revelatory expression of divinity in the flow of history.[2] Hence the words of Jesus drew the greatest attention. Narrative frameworks were secondary and only gradually were emphases distinct to one particular gospel recognised.

Whilst a primacy was given to Jesus' words, a complex enclosure was erected about the woman. It reflected the gender contests of society and church. Access to higher education, maternal responses to children and to Jesus, patterns of simple piety and humility, even feminine eating pat-

---

1. RA Harrisville, 'The Woman of Canaan: A Chapter in the History of Exegesis', in *Interpretation* 20 (1966): 286.
2. See S Briggs, 'The Deceit of the Sublime: An Investigation into the Origins of Ideological Criticism of the Bible in Early Nineteenth-Century German Biblical Studies', in *Semeia* 59 (1992): 12–13.

terns were all inscribed on the Syrophoenician's word and her body by spermatothanic ink.³

European missiological and commercial concerns were spliced into the interpretative process. Ethnicity and conversion, fascination with 'oriental curiosities' and an evolutionist construction of the march of civilisation provided a rationale for focus on this pericope and a discourse field for its exposition. This paper aims to explore the immense Syrophoenician superstructure as a means of demonstrating that cultural and political contests are enmeshed with and justified by doctrinal and ecclesial claims.

The Beginnings of Critical Enquiry

Early critical forays into the story were controlled by the conflict between orthodoxy and dogmatic Christology on the one hand and the demands of historical-critical enquiry. In this debate, the first set of Jesus' words was the focus of attention.⁴

Various explanations for the response of the 'earthly Jesus' were offered. Some counted the offence of Jesus' words as a criterion of authenticity.⁵ However, the offence was ameliorated, assigned to Jesus' Jewish background rather than his own dominical authority,⁶ especially when classified as a 'proverb'.⁷ Dogmatic orthodoxy required that Jesus 'con-

---

3. See Helena Michie, *The Flesh Made Word: Female Figures and Women's Bodies* (New York/Oxford: Oxford University Press, 1987), 124–50.
4. Only in 1890 did William Aldis Wright interpret the differences between Matthew and Mark in the *second* response of Jesus as significant. He asserted that these were theologically motivated but neglected to provide the explanation; see his *The Composition of the Four Gospels* (London: Macmillan & Co, 1890), 137.
5. The problem of their omission from Luke's gospel had not yet arisen.
6. D Smith, 'Our Lord's Hard Saying to the Syrophoenician Woman' in *Expository Times* 12 (1901): 319. The argument from offence to authenticity is also found in FW Farrar, *The Life of Christ* (London: Cassell & Co, nd. [c. 1875]), 366. See also RW Dale, 'The Syrophoenician Woman' in *The Expositor* 5th Series, 5 (1897): 365. Ernest Renan however, regarded the Gentile mission as inextricably part of the Jesus' universal vision *as a Jew: Vie de Jésus* (Paris: Calmann-Lévy, 3rd edition, nd. [1st edition, 1861]), 237. This suited his cultivation of a Christian theme of universal brotherhood: 'La fraternité humaine dans le sens le plus large sortait à pleins bords de tous ses enseignements' (241).
7. Smith, 'Hard Saying', 320, drawing on the collection of proverbs mustered by Erasmus. The same argument is retained by Augustine Stock, *The Method and Message of Mark* (Wilmington, DE: Michael Glazier, 1989), 213. The possibility of a common proverb of the ilk 'Charity begins at home' had already been mooted by EH Plumptre, *The Gospel According to St. Mark* (Ellicott's New Testament Commentary) (London: Cassell & Co, nd. [c.1870]), 93. Isaac Williams called it a proverbial saying similar to 'Give not that

trolled the affair . . . [including undertaking] the whole journey for her sake.'⁸ Jesus' words, far from being offensive, were designed either to rebuke the woman for being 'unseasonably importunate'⁹ or to cultivate her faith. If the former, the male disciples were exonerated by the woman's culpability; if the latter, the disciples were adjudged to be in need of training—the woman transmogrified into the Teacher's lesson-plan.¹⁰

Domination by Matthean Emphases

Matthew was relied upon to sanitise Mark's text. Even if source-critical debates[11] were disturbing Augustinian orthodoxy, Matthean *interpretative* dominance still reigned.[12] For the Scottish nonconformist, James Mori-

---

which is holy to the dogs' (Mt 7:6, 2 Pet 2:22): *Devotional Commentary on the Gospel Narrative: Our Lord's Ministry (The Third Year)* (London: Rivingtons, 1870), 23.

8. JA and ME Bengel and JCF Stendel, *Gnomon of the New Testament* translated by J Bandinei (Edinburgh: T&T Clark, 1877), Volume 1, 528. This is a nineteenth century English translation of an eighteenth century writing, noteworthy for the number of additions made by the translator as well as the continued popularity and influence of Bengel's tome, described by AB Bruce as 'unique': 'The Synoptic Gospels' in *The Expositor's Greek Testament* (London: Hodder and Stoughton, 2ⁿᵈ edition, 1901) Volume 1, 390.

9. Bengel 529. GA Chadwick, *The Gospel of St. Mark* (London: Hodder & Stoughton, 1903), 196. Compare however Henry Cowan who, after a series of intertextual connections which made the story all about men's interests, allocates one female distinctive to the story: women unlike men are sympathetic to importunity—as also God: 'Syrophoenician Woman', in J Hasting, JA Selbie and JC Lambert (editors), *A Dictionary of Christ and the Gospels* (Edinburgh: T&T Clark, 1906), Volume 2, 693.

10. Albert Barnes, *Notes on the New Testament* (London: Blackie & Son, 1832), 161, H Olshausen, *Biblical Commentary on the Gospels* (Clark's Foreign Theological Library Volume X) (Edinburgh: T&T Clark, 1848), Volume 2, 204, AE Garvie, 'Studies in the 'Inner Life' of Jesus: The Scope of the Ministry', *The Expositor* 6ᵗʰ Series, 6 (1902): 306; Alfred Edersheim disputes this motivation of Jesus but nonetheless makes the woman a foil for the teaching of Jesus about the nature of his own Messiahship which she was to come to believe, as the effective cause of the child's cure: *The Life and Times of Jesus the Messiah* (Grand Rapids: Eerdmans, 1972 [repr. 1883, 1886]), Volume 2, 40.

11. See JC O'Neill, *The Bible's Authority: A Portrait Gallery of Thinkers from Lessing to Bultmann* (Edinburgh: T&T Clark, 1991), 123.

12. Some commentators on Mk 7:24-30, immediately refer the reader to the notes on Mt 15:21-28; see, for example, JH Blunt, *The Annotated Bible: Being a Household Commentary upon Holy Scripture* (London: Rivingtons, 1882), Volume 3, 125. EH Plumptre's notes on St Mark's Gospel in CJ Ellicott's *New Testament Commentary for English Readers* (London: Cassell, 1901 [c 1870]) reduced Mark to little more than a fly-leaf between Matthew and Luke by his constant referring of the reader to his notes on the

son, 'The Lord [in Mark] ... previously told the suppliant that his ... was a mission to the children of Israel.' Alfred Edersheim determined that Jesus did not leave Israel.[13] The concerns governing this interpretation of Jesus were shadowed by revolutions in Europe. For Henry Wace, Jesus was the exemplary law-abiding citizen-son: 'His ministry was governed by certain laws which had been determined for purposes of the highest import, and it was no easy matter for Him to depart from them.'[14] The merciful exemption was evidence that he was making the faith of the woman patent for her own benefit or for onlookers.[15] Turned from 'unseasonable importunacy', the woman now underscored Jesus' wisdom-words, her own utterance a christological proof. Matthean faith not Markan word dominated both gospels.[16]

History and the power of the idea

History as Providence and the Privileging of Jesus' Position

History, especially in English manipulation, was the servant of belief.[17] Though the days of deriving all history from the biblical record were passing, there

---

first gospel parallel.
13. J Morison explicitly cross-referenced Mt 15:24: *Mark's Memoirs of Jesus Christ: Or A Commentary on the Gospel According to Mark* (London: Hamilton, Adams & Co, 2nd edition, 1876), 211. Alfred Edersheim also argues on the basis of Matthew that in Mark's account, Jesus cannot have left the boundaries of Israel and that he stayed in a Jewish home (for Passover no less—2.38); so also Olshausen, 2.202 and n1.
14. Henry Wace, quoted in *The Expository Times* 4 (1892-93): 81; in the same collation is a similar comment from Alexander Maclaren. The teacher, and son of an Archbishop of Canterbury, Arthur Benson, argued from obedience to God to obedience to society's rules, no doubt with some of his recalcitrant schoolboy charges in mind: '... if they are true to the spirit of Christ, they have no concern with revolutionary concerns at all; Christ's own example teaches us to leave all that on one side, to conform to worldly institutions, to accept the framework of society.' *From a College Window* (London: Smith, Elder & Co, 1906), 320.
15. 'Christ descends to her ground that He may raise her from it.' Such was Dale's interpretation ('The Syrophoenician Woman', 370); *cf.* Olshausen: 'In this mode then of Christ's giving an answer to prayer we are to trace only another form of his love.' (2.204).
16. The social commentator, poet and Oxford churchman, Isaac Williams, argues for the benefits of harmonising the two accounts,: Williams, 21.
17. This conception had a marked tenacity. When a proposed collection of essays titled *The Church—Past and Present* was promoted in a pamphlet by HM Gwatkin, it was stated, 'We write not as advocates of this or that party in Church or State, but as students who are persuaded that history even more than science is the special message of the Spirit to our time.' (Enclosure in letter HM Gwatkin to J Armitage Robinson, 9/5/1898; Westminster Abbey Library Archives, Armitage Robinson collection.)

remained a privileging of the 'history' in the Gospels over any other evidence that might surface from the surrounding time.[18] Hence socio-cultural/-historical concerns were rarely cited, except where some difficulty was felt, especially with Jesus' words.[19] The woman's cultural background, wisdom and character did not rise from the ground.

History and Tradition: the Broad Lines of Conflict

The avowal of history as providence was, however, problematic in the nineteenth century. At one end of the spectrum, stood the inheritance of Idealism. Renan, for example, claimed that 'the Ideal endures, and is; and the Material, which seems to be, is but fleeting and perishes.'[20] The 'Material', for more radical interpreters, might even be found to have 'coloured' the Gospels. At the other end, longevity of historical witness became the all, especially as a support for ecclesial partisanship.[21]

---

18. JA Froude, 'Criticism and the Gospel History', in his *Short Studies on Great Subjects* (London: Longmans, Green and Co, 1893), Volume 1, 253–4. Thus, the evidence of Josephus must bow to that provided by the Gospels: BF Westcott, *Introduction to the Study of the Gospels* (New York: EP Dutton, 1875), 389. There was a censor, however, reinforcing the acceptable borders of history. The control of enquiry exercised by the Established Church, such as over the contributors to the watershed collection, *Essays & Reviews* (published 1860) added a costliness to critical enquiry that tempered enthusiasm. But this was not unknown in Germany either: the 'Judas' deviancy label hounded Strauss from his university appointment; see B Kaye, 'DF Strauss and the European Theological Tradition: Der Ischariotismus unsere Tag?' *Journal of Religious History* 17 (1992): 172–93. Even so, the mere suggestion that an English theologian might be 'Germanic' was enough to generate considerable suspicion. Westcott, for example, who early sought to bring attention to the movements in Germany (such as the writings of FC Baur), appears to have suffered from his willingness to engage the new currents (JB Lightfoot to Westcott 15/8/1861, 5/10/1861, 'Lightfoot Letters', Dean and Chapter Library, Durham Cathedral).
19. Martin Kähler saw through this self-deception: 'The exclusiveness with which we are referred to Christian sources must certainly arouse suspicion outside the Christian circle of vision.' *Der sogennante historische Jesus und der geschichtliche, biblische Christus* (Leipzig: A Deichert, 2nd edition, 1896), translated by CE Braaten as *The So-called Historical Jesus and the Historic Biblical Christ* (Philadelphia: Fortress Press, 1988), 49n7. This did not drive Kähler to embrace cultural considerations however; he simply recognised the necessary consequence of embracing an historical approach. He felt that such cultural asides that were beginning to gain favour in nineteenth century Biblical interpretation were distractions from the central import of the Gospels (70).
20. Quoted in AD Hallowell (editor), *James and Lucretia Mott:Life and Letters* (Boston: Houghton, Mifflin and Co, 1884), frontispiece.
21. Kähler also used the argument of longevity, but focussed upon the ongoing proclamation of faith by Christians through the centuries as testimony to the pre-eminence of faith as the criterion of assessment of Jesus (95, 102). For a useful overview of the emphases of the period, see S Prickett, 'Romantics and Victorians: from Typology to Symbolism', in S Prickett (editor), *Reading the Text: Biblical Criticism and Literary Theory*

Midway were those of a liberal persuasion who, under a developing theologising of the incarnation, refused to separate the Ideal from the Real. A carefully-drawn interpretative continuum from the fathers onwards witnessed to the gospel's historical verities, frequently paring away perceived traditional accretions. Whichever approach was adopted, the claim was grounded in the stability of language.

Language and Idea: Sanitising Jesus' Words

Language *and* its grammar, even more than its literature, were the keys to access the truth behind or unfolding in history.[22] When the Syrophoenician was interpreted as 'woman', an implicit reliance upon an essentialist and natural meaning emerged from classical etymology or comparative philology.[23] Language described the world rather than constructed

---

(Oxford: Blackwell, 1991), 182-224.

22. Elisabeth Schüssler Fiorenza's perception that language is not 'natural' but the result of a grammatical construction system highlights the nineteenth century mainstream accent that grammar and language were compatriots in the demonstration of reality: *Jesus: Miriam's Child, Sophia's Prophet: Critical Issues in Feminist Christology* (London: SCM, 1995), 161–62. Both grammar and language were constructed to demonstrate a particular reality. Poor grammar, syntax and spelling were thus an offence against the truth. For some, it demonstrated class, gender and racial hierarchies; for others, it promoted limited access to training. This was why (some) women could be encouraged to study Latin! It was not for Latin's own sake, but that they might better understand English: F Gadesden, 'Secondary Education of Girls and the Development of Girls' High Schools' in RD Roberts (editor), *Education in the Nineteenth Century: Lectures delivered in the Education Section of the Cambridge University Extension Summer Meeting in August 1900* (Cambridge: at the University Press, 1901), 86. But this cannot be reduced to utilitarian design. Westcott, for example, regarded the learning of grammar as a *moral* exercise. Such morality harboured its own gender politics as the grammatical systems that inscribed the female to the exceptional, exerted their hold over the development of modern English. See J Penelope, *Speaking Freely: Unlearning the Lies of the Father's Tongues* (New York: Pergamon Press, 1990). Thus Latin for women, as an aid to modern English, functioned not merely as training in language but as a linguistic reinforcement of the ordered state of women. Compare P Demers, *Women as Interpreters of the Bible* (New York: Paulist Press, 1992), 94–96. Not all women however accepted the male version of the essentialism of language (see Selvidge, *infra*).
23. JW Donaldson, one of the earliest proponents of the importance of history to the study of language, might rail against the position that there is 'no truth except so far as it is presented under certain forms of speech or modes of thought' but he simultaneously held Christianity could be defended by its 'inherent truth and historical certainty': *Christian Orthodoxy: Reconciled with the Conclusions of Modern Biblical Learning: A Theological Essay, with Critical and Controversial Supplements* (London: Williams &

one.[24] As Brooke Foss Westcott declared: 'I confess . . . to . . . an absolute faith in language and so in Scripture.'[25]

Given that it was the providential, divine Jesus, his use of the diminutive κυνάρια became pedagogical, even playful in intent. Lexicons therefore were constrained to indicate this 'pure vision of the truth'. Marla Selvidge's recent study of the keen interest of nineteenth century feminists in language, asserts that 'people who compile grammars and lexicons have a philosophical predisposition concerning how meaning should be derived'.[26] Κυνάριον provides a potent example. The 1791 lexicon of Johannes Schleusner delivered the meanings: a lapdog plaything, a distinction from the intimidating Molossian hound (and thence to a 'miniature' of κύων). Noteworthy is his restriction of the New Testament usage to the degrading and contemptuous term for a person.[27] But within half a century, the lexical entry had become standardised as a value-free, even positive diminutive.[28] By the turn of the twentieth century, Friedrich Blass was arguing for its classification as an 'endearing term'.[29] For David Smith, any suggestion that Jesus 'had hitherto shared the narrow prejudices of His time and race' was 'less than reverent, nor is it consistent with the

---

Norgate, 1857), vi–vii.

24. See Nancy Rabinowitz, 'Introduction' in NS Rabinowitz and A Richlin (editors), *Feminist Theory and the Classics* (New York: Routledge, 1993), 3–6 for contemporary perpetuations of such understandings and their political consequences.
25. BF Westcott to MacMillan, 9/12/1859, British Library, Add Ms 55,092, f 73.
26. MJ Selvidge, *Notorious Voices: Feminist Biblical Interpretation 1500-1920* (London: SCM Press, 1996), 213.
27. *designandi hominem abjectum et contemtibilem*: JF Schleusner, *Novum Lexicon Graeco-Latinum in Novum Testamentum* (Glasgow: A&J Duncan, 4th edition, 1817 [1791]), Volume 1, 963. See also JH Bass, *Greek-English Lexicon to the New Testament* (London: George Bell and Sons, 4th edition, 1878 [1829]), 129 which gives the only meaning as 'cur', a relic from the previous century; compare ST Bloomfield, *The Greek Testament with English Notes* (London: Longman, Brown, Green and Longmans, 6th edition, 1845), Volume 1, 216: 'The diminutive is, as often, expressive of contempt.'
28. HG Liddell and R Scott, *A Greek-English Lexicon Based on the German Work of Francis Passow* (Oxford: University Press, 2nd edition, 1845 [1843]), sv.; CG Wilke, *Clavis Novi Testamenti Philologica* (Leipzig: Arnold, 1850), Volume 1, 627, followed by JH Thayer, *A Greek-English Lexicon of the New Testament* (Edinburgh: T&T Clark, 2nd edition, 1890) sv.
29. F Blass, *Grammar of New Testament Greek* translated by H St John Thackeray (London: Macmillan, 1898), 64. Bandinei's footnote to the 1877 edition of Bengel's *Gnomon* asserts the same (310).

facts',[30] and he collared Origen in support,[31] through it smothering any cultural distinctives between Jew and Greek.[32] Visual reinforcement in family bibles tailored reading directions, even with a distinctly gentrified ambience.[33] Philology had been made to serve dogma.

Linguistics and History: an uneasy alliance

The irony was that the nineteenth century fascination with the 'East'[34] was undermining the 'historically' defended linguistic turn. James Morison, relying on testimony from travellers to Palestine, acknowledged the general Jewish antipathy towards dogs. He resolved the tension with the sentimental observation that 'There is in the dog, . . . a deep instinct of yearning for human society . . . a chord in their nature that becomes readily responsive to human kindness . . . there can be no doubt that in ancient times children and little dogs would get into terms of good fellowship.'[35]

---

30. Smith, 'Hard Saying', 320. Smith had adopted an 'idealistic' approach to Jesus, conceiving him to be 'the ideal of humanity' immeasurably beyond even the reporters of his life: 'Recent New Testament Criticism: The Supreme Evidence of the Historicity of the Evangelic Jesus', *The Expositor* 6th Series, 4 (1901): 289-94. Ezra Gould held that Jesus was simply expressing a commonly held (Jewish) opinion, not his own: *A Critical and Exegetical Commentary on the Gospel of Mark* (ICC) (Edinburgh: T&T Clark, 1896), 136. The suggestion that Smith criticises is found especially in those 'Lives of Jesus' which adopted what was called at the time, a psychological developmental approach to Jesus life; see, for example, Garvie, 297.
31. HB Swete, *The Gospel According to St. Mark* (London: Macmillan, 2nd edition, 1902, [1898]), 157; A Plummer *The Gospel According to St Mark* (Cambridge: University Press, 1914), 189.
32. Ulrich Luz has recognised the first world's sometimes exaggerated love of dogs as an influence on interpretation: *Matthew 8-20* (Hermeneia) translated by JE Crouch (Minneapolis: Fortress Press, 2001), 340.
33. For example, the nineteenth century *Illustrated Family Bible* published by Cassell, Petter and Galpin of London and New York (nd.).
34. See generally, AH Cadwallader and M Trainor, 'The rise and fall of the European recovery of the Ancient site of Colossae' in *International Symposium on the History and Culture of Denizli and its Surroundings* (Denizli: Pamukkale University, 2007), Volume 2, 73-79.
35. Morison, 212, drawing on JG Wood, *Bible Animals: being a description of every living creature mentioned in the Scriptures from the ape to the coral* (London: Longmans, 1869). The translation given by Bp MacEvilly ('dogs' for κυνάρια in Jesus' words but 'whelps' in the woman's reply), may indicate some sensitivity at least to the different intent behind the speaker's usage: *An Exposition of the Gospels* (Dublin: WB Kelly, 2nd edition, 1877), Volume 1, 635. There is however, one brief note hidden in Dean Farrar's *Life of Christ* that remained singularly undeveloped in its potential for a reading

Thus the 'little' in the diminutive form became 'young', no longer belittling. The comparison of a woman with a dog, implied *she* had 'a deep instinct for human society'. The ethological comparison ends up being confirmed by the exposition:[36] the woman and her daughter are dogs, yearning for (hu)man community. No matter that the infantilising diminutive gained a bestial metonymy. AB Bruce responded that faith turned a dog into a child![37]

History was fettered to grammar and to 'great' literature as the primary resource for the discovery of the Idea(l). The text, or conceivably the speech which lay behind it, brought the coalescence of language and history. Materiality was secondary and held at bay if it threatened to challenge either the Idea(l) or its historical defence. Language as the bearer of culture was a secondary consideration if it existed at all. Language as a linguistic system, the result of culture, was too radical a proposition.[38] The barest of general cultural information that came at this time reflected other nineteenth century European interests: mission and commerce.

Ethnicity and Subjection to Missionary Civilisation

The Syrophoenician woman's story was torn by European protagonists in the manifold directions of debates about history and the idea. The recovery of a name for her and her daughter (Justa and Bernice)[39] was little

---

  of dialogue from a cultural perspective. In a footnote to his discussion of the passage, Farrar writes, 'To a Jew (as Mr Kenrick has reminded me) a dog was the object of the utmost contempt and abhorrence, as it is at this day to the Mohammedans: whereas with the Greeks it was, perhaps as often as ourselves, a household pet . . . ' However rather than admit that this might forge a separation between Jesus the Jew and the Gentile woman, Farrar interprets the dialogue in the light of this comment, to prove that Jesus was testing her faith 'that He might crown it with a more complete and glorious reward'. Thus, for him, there is 'the peculiar aptitude of our Lord's answer and of this foreigner's retort.' (368); compare also HM Luckock, *Footprints of the Son of Man as Traced by Saint Mark* (London: Rivingtons, 2nd edition, 1885), 262 and JS Exell, *The Biblical Illustrator: St. Mark* (London: James Nisbet, nd.), 291; Chadwick, *St Mark*, 198.
36. On the ethological dimensions of the story, see my *Beyond the Word of a Woman: Recovering the Bodies of the Syrophoenician Women* (Adelaide: ATF Press, 2008).
37. AB Bruce, *The Kingdom of God* (Edinburgh: T&T Clark, 1897), 107-8—an unwitting variation on the *Catena in Acta (Catena Andreae)* 176.6 where the woman (as dog) is turned into an ἄνθρωπος.
38. Even though not unknown in the nineteenth century: see E Blondel, *Nietzsche: The Body and Culture: Philosophy as a Philological Genealogy* translated by S Hand (London: The Athlone Press, 1991).
39. See my 'What's in a Name? The Tenacity of a Tradition of Interpretation [Justus/a and

more than a historicist curio,[40] akin to European inquisitiveness (acquisitiveness?) about the rediscovered 'East'. Whatever the 'historical' interest, no subjectivity was granted the woman, except insofar as she might become an honourable mother who made her daughter's suffering her own.

The nineteenth century witnessed massive European missiological endeavours, tracking trade routes.[41] The resultant interest in 'oriental cities' cultivated greater expansiveness on the opening of the Markan pericope,[42] even swamping its entire meaning.[43] Comments on Tyre and Sidon's opulence, idolatry and commerce were foregrounded.[44] Such paltry cultural consciousness was driven by apologetic purposes; the Church in this instance was 'in the loins' of Jesus, exorcising heathen nations as it christianised those with whom trade had been established.[45] Her Greek ethnicity (7:26) became her *religious* background.[46] The woman had to leave behind her idolatrous and pagan practices, especially given their consequences of the daughter's demonic possession, in order to come to Jesus.[47]

---

the Clementine Homilies]' Festschrift for Victor Pfitzner, edited by P Lockwood, *Lutheran Theological Journal* 39 (2005): 218–39.

40. Swete, *Mark* 157; Cowan, 693; Luckock, *Footprints*, 260.
41. The consciousness of contemporary missions in connection with the Syrophoenician's story is clearly seen in Dale, 'The Syrophoenician Woman', 367.
42. And at this stage, only a few commentators were rejecting 'and Sidon' from the text of 7:24. Even though Tischendorf's edition of the Greek New Testament had dropped it, the editions in nineteenth century use—Griesbach, Mill, Scholz, Scrivener and even Tregelles (though with a marginal note) —retained it.
43. See, for example, Plumptre, 'St Mark', 208–9.
44. Morison, 209, Gould, *Mark*, 134–5, Farrar, *Life of Christ*, 369; compare Swete, *Mark*, 159.
45. 'Beyond [Tyre and Sidon] was the blue expanse of the Mediterranean, over which the messengers of the gospel were to bear its glad tidings to the centers of the world's great empire.' EG White, *The Desire of Ages* (Melbourne: Echo Publishing Co, 1903), 399, in a none-too-subtle collation of the Roman and British empires! India is evoked as the prime mission field addressed by this passage in her comment that 'caste is hateful to God' (403). Alternately, with the focus given to the civilisation which accompanied the missionary enterprise, GA Chadwick deduced, 'Thus Jesus really domesticated the Gentile world.' (*Mark*, 198).
46. E Stapfer *Le Nouveau Testament* (Paris: Librairie Fischbacher, 1889), 149n4. Note, however, that Swete sees the reference as indicating a 'Greek-speaker' (*Mark*, 157). The shift from 'Greek' to 'heathen' (as in H Alford, *The Greek Testament* (London: Rivington's, 1856), Volume 1, 155) expanded the missiological dimensions of the story for nineteenth century interests.
47. Bernard Weiss reduces such demonic possession to 'the result of their moral condition': *The Life of Christ* translated by JW Hope (Edinburgh: T&T Clark, 3 Volumes, 1883), 2.81.

Missiological categories of christian and heathen, with unequal values attached to each, were thus hidden under the guise of scholarly historical enquiry and adherence to dogma. As heathen to the Church, as accidental moment to providential history, so was the woman to Jesus.

The woman became a type of the Gentile church,[48] a paradigm indebted to patristic and Anglo-Saxon interpretation.[49] By a myopic lexical focus Ἑλληνίς meant 'Gentile' rather than 'Greek'.[50] Τῷ γένει was unquestioned as the woman's racial descent (and hence, quite reconcilable with the Matthean 'Canaanite'). The Vulgate had effectively sealed the typology, by providing *gentilis*, rather than the translation *graeca* of some Old Latin manuscripts.[51] Such had passed into the earliest English translation —Wycliffe's 'hethene'. Hence, just as grammatically feminine forms were determined by masculine usage, so also the woman yielded her gendered specificity to a generalised ecclesial typology.

For some, missiology was reinforced by the philosophy of evolution, an inevitable movement coursing through his-

---

48. Or alternately, of all idolators, in which case the text was used to demonstrate that Christ 'was the Saviour, not only of the Jews, but of the whole human race . . .'. ST Bloomfield, *Recensio Synoptica Annotationis Sacrae* (London: C&J Rivington, 1826), Volume 2, 61. Regardless of the nuance, the end result for the woman was the same— gender was lost in Gentile idolatry. Such was the dreary focus of two lengthy sermons on the Syrophoenician woman by Samuel Horsley, Bishop of Asaph; see his *Sermons* (Dundee: James Chalmers, 1812), 134–74.
49. The Venerable Bede, for example, commented, 'Symbolically, this gentile woman . . . denotes the church gathered from the gentiles.' (Bede 2.7 [*PL* 92 202A-B]).
50. Swete, *Mark*, 156, Gould, *Mark*, 135, Plumptre, 'St Mark', 208. JB Lightfoot, *On a Fresh Revision of the English New Testament* (London: Macmillan, 1872), 157n1. Other commentators adopted a literary approach and saw in the use of Ἑλληνίς an example of synecdoche or metonymy, that is 'Greek' was the part signifying the whole, or was the characteristic emblem representing the larger entity: see Morison, 211; Gould by contrast simply reads the word as 'Gentile', Syrophoenician being the particular expression of it (135).
51. For example, a b c d. The influence of the Old Latin and Vulgate versions and Western patristic commentators on interpretation of the text is quite significant in the definition of the parameters of meaning: see Bengel, 529. Breaking the hold of the Latin was one of the key scholarly achievements of the nineteenth century and this applied as much to Scriptural as Classical studies. However, the asides in Bloomfield demonstrate how strong was the continued hold of the Vulgate: see Bloomfield, *Greek Testament*, 1.216.

tory. Bernard Weiss is quite clear: 'this view of heathen as an elementary religion corresponding to the child age of mankind already points to a future, in which the divine education of the human race would develop this into religious manhood.'[52] No concerns about gender intruded here, except insofar as (christian) man was confirmed by evolution as the superior. Renan avoided any mention of the woman: 'the Pagan may obtain grace, provided he have faith, is humble and recognises the precedence of the son of the house.'[53]

Even with the introduction of cultural elements, prior ideological commitments governed inclusion and interpretation. In sum, 'word' remained by and large quarantined from specific cultural context, which might, dangerously, particularise the man of Palestine.

History on the Verge of Independent Narrative

The *assertion* of history as providential in itself suggests that there were resistant notions of history. The genealogical interest, that is, the tracing of the lines of development of ideas and institutions to their origins, could not only be used to prise away the immobilising rust of tradition even as it retained a claim to longevity. It could also develop history's own discrete authority, where the narrative of history was not viewed as coextensive with the narrative of faith.

The basis was laid for a clash of narratives or a stand-off. David Strauss claimed warrant from Mark's Gospel itself. He argued Mark was not guided by considerations of history, but rather potential offence, when he softened the Matthean text delimiting Jesus' mission to the lost sheep of the house of Israel. Jesus shared the antipathy of his countrymen towards Gentiles, and his reply to the woman had no interest in exhilarating her

---

52. B Weiss, *The Religion of the New Testament*, translated by GH Schodde (New York/London: Funk & Wagnalls, 1905), 166-7. The comment also indicates the extent to which the extolling of 'masculine Christianity' had spread through Europe. 'Masculine' or 'male' in this context was associated with the stage beyond primitive religion. 'Child' (and one wonders where woman was placed) was assimilated with primitive.
53. E Renan, *The History of the Origins of Christianity Book V: The Gospels* (London: Mathieson & Co, nd.), 61. He compares Acts 10.

faith.⁵⁴ Consequently, the Gentile mission and the emphasis on faith were the church's development.⁵⁵

The response to the individuation of history was either to seek its reconnection with the Jesus of the text or to renounce the control that history exerted on the lines of faith. Without predetermining that history must reinforce dogma, the Cambridge triumvirate of Westcott, Lightfoot and Hort worked for the reintegration of history, text and the Idea(l). The German, Martin Kähler, however, sought to make faith independent of historical research. His twin in England was Benjamin Jowett, who sponsored a literary reading of the text—interpreting the bible as any other work of literature.⁵⁶ This was little more than a variation on the positing of the supreme Idea which may or may not be recognised in history, literature or philosophy (depending on the stance one adopted). At this stage there was little analysis of form or detail of the very words that were the governing concern in the interpretation of the passage. Word still held a hegemonic sway over the words. For both options, the passage was simply a large clay pigeon in a shooting contest on closed estates.

However, that there was a contest, that there were competitors whose shots were beginning to be heard in broader acres, was awakening the possibility that there was no longer, and perhaps no longer need for, a 'common objective reality'.⁵⁷ Women were among a number who took advantage from this development,⁵⁸ though almost a century would pass before that became clear.

---

54. He points to the ease of a narrative insertion along the lines of Jn 6:6 (admittedly running counter to Markan style, which was a category of perspective barely acknowledged at this point).
55. Strauss, 301–3.
56. Kähler, 70. B Jowett, 'The Interpretation of Scripture' in *Essays and Reviews* (London: Longman, Green, Longman & Roberts, 1861), 370. Similar was Matthew Arnold; see my 'Male Diagnosis of the Female Pen in the late Victorian Britain: Private Assessments of Supernatural Religion', in *Journal of Anglican Studies* 5 (2007): 67–86.
57. Prickett, 220.
58. Mark Freed argues that Mary Ward in her novel about the crisis of faith in Victorian England, *Robert Elsmere*, works for an acknowledgement of 'alternative articulations of spiritual and moral truth': 'The Moral Irrelevance of Dogma: Mary Ward and Critical Theology in England' in J Melnyk (editor), *Women's Theology in Nineteenth-Century Britain: Transfiguring the Faith of Their Fathers* (New York: Garland Publishing, 1998), 140.

Anti-semitism as a Technique in Commentary

With the focus on the word as bearer of the idea, it was usually the idea (in its interpretative exposition) that counted. Occasionally, somewhat closer attention attended Jesus' opening words: ἄφες πρῶτον χορτασθῆναι τὰ τέκνα (7:27). Here Pauline influences guided the interpretation[59] with 'first' now softening harsher views.

This was less interested in correcting the centuries-long anti-semitic tendencies congealed on this passage.[60] Gentile supremacy was simply taken for granted.[61] Firstly, it justified hierarchies of place and access to privilege in the commentator's own time. One paraphrase of Jesus' words ran thus: 'Do not ask me before the time to confer benefits upon you, nor act like servants who would be fed before the children are satiated.'[62] Secondly, the inherited anti-semitic dispensationalist interpretations[63] were turned to ferocious contemporary battles.

The Cambridge Professor of Modern History, JR Seeley, compared the thought-control by one particular party in Judaism with the oppressive fusion of theology, law, academia and literature in England against the writers of *Essays and Reviews* and against Bishop Colenso.[64] Jesus' retreat

---

59. Weiss, *Life*, 3.38n1; Bruce, 'Synoptic Gospels', 390.
60. There were nevertheless some retentions of ancient abuse. Exell wrote of 'the Jews, whose first care was to hate, to mock and to curse all besides themselves . . . ' (291). John M'Farlane provided comments to one family Holy Bible: 'not in any degree proselyted to the Jewish religion' (Glasgow: William Collins, Sons & Co, nd [1865]), 49; Swete is reminded of the exchange of the language of abuse (that is, 'dogs') that was engineered by some of the Church Fathers, such as Jerome (*Mark*, 158). On this interpretation, Jews, because of their rejection of Jesus, took the place of the outsiders and hence now were the dogs. See JB Lightfoot, *St. Paul's Epistle to the Philippians* (London: Macmillan, 12th edition, 1898 [1868]), 143–4. Lightfoot's paraphrase of Paul's intent in Phil 3:2 ('Beware of the dogs . . . ') deliberately evokes Mk 7:1–30 in its disputed combination of purity concerns ('the washing of cups and platters') with dining access ('God's children . . . eating at the God's table').
61. Frederick Farrar's introduction to his *Life of Christ* directly addresses Jews. There is no hint of aggressive anti-semitism. Indeed there is an acknowledgement of past Christian horrors visited upon Jews, of which the present age was unworthy. At the same time, wafting through the glow of decorous language is the unmistakable mark of Victorian self-confidence (xi-xii).
62. Chr Friedrich Fritzsche quoted by Bloomfield, *Greek Testament*, 1.216.
63. Seen for example in Tertullian, *On Prayer*, 6.3.
64. Seeley's *Ecce Homo*, published originally in 1866, kept its authorship hidden from the public for a number of editions. This was no doubt a protection from the weight of ecclesiological conservatism that, with the full weight of an established church polity, harnessed judicial and political investigation to control the burgeoning liberalism in

into the hinterland of Tyre (and Sidon) became an escape from a Pharisaical conspiracy, seething after Jesus' triumphant critique of Jewish scruples (Mk 7:1–23).[65]

More popularly acceptable, the 'wall of division' between Jew and Gentile heard in the story became that between christian and heathen, further sounding the missiological clarion-call.[66] The Jew was rendered invisible, except as a grotesque, distorted foil for gospel truth.

Reconciling all these readings is impossible. What is clear is that the Syrophoenician woman's story was at the mercy of contests over a number of nineteenth century positions. One further looms large.

Gender as a problem

More important than reconstructions of a Jewish backdrop to this story was the portrayal of the woman, though an expression of the equality of salvation between women and men is rare.[67] The standard characterisation of the Syrophoenician clearly demarcated the values recommended

---

biblical and theological studies. Strikingly, when Ernest Renan's *Life of Jesus* was first translated into English from the French, these national religious controversies were explicitly named in the Preface (again, anonymously) as belonging to the same sentiments raised about Renan's work, that is, of the battles between the 'obscurantists' and those who wish 'to preserve the religious spirit, whilst getting rid of the superstitions and absurdities that deform it, and which are alike opposed to science and common sense' (vii-viii). Bishop Colenso was the Church of England Bishop of Natal, who, having learned from the Zulus that the hare does not chew the cud (in contradiction to Deut 14:7) began questioning much of the literalist understanding of the Old Testament record in his *The Pentateuch and Book of Joshua Critically Examined*. He was tried for heresy in an English court and dismissed from his office. See generally, O Chadwick, *The Victorian Church 1829–1859* (London: SCM Press, 3rd edition, 1971), 544-53.

65. Plumptre, 'St. Mark', 99, Chadwick *St. Mark* 195, Gould, *Mark* 134, Swete, *Mark* 155, Lindsay 269: 'spying Scribes and Pharisees'; White, *Desire of Ages* 401: 'scribes and Pharisees desiring to take his life'. Seeley attempted to preserve anonymity of authorship through at least six editions!
66. For example, White, *Desire of Ages*, 402–3.
67. C Schmidt's *Social Results of Christianity* translated by M Thorpe (London: Wm. Isbister, 1885), 140) is the only work I have discovered which cites the Canaanite / Syrophoenician story as warrant for this general assertion, often made polemically in other contexts by male commentators reminding their (imagined?) female audience that, compared to ancient oppressions, they never had it so good! By contrast, Mrs EG White in her gathering of citations to demonstrate the removal of distinctions in Christ, footnotes Gal 3:28 but somehow neglects to include 'neither male nor female' in her rendition (compare 1 Cor 12:13): *Desire of Ages*, 403 and n2.

for women by men. Charlotte Gilman, the nineteenth century American feminist, devastatingly critiqued the dominant construction: 'This ultra littleness and ultra femaleness has been demanded and produced by our Androcentric Culture.'[68] This minority position must be kept in mind as the hegemonic discourse is analysed.

The Ideal Woman as Humble, Homely and Maternal

The humility of the mother became necessary, honourable and proper to an encounter with (the man) Jesus. John M'Farlane's editorial notes to one popular family bible in the 1860s waxed sermonically:

> Those that would obtain mercy from Christ, must throw themselves at his feet; must refer themselves to him, humble themselves before him, and give themselves up to be ruled by him.[69]

The irony was that this nineteenth century Christian freedom was modelled upon the ancient world of Greece and Rome.[70] As Sarah Pomeroy writes: 'Self-sacrifice or martyrdom is the standard way for a woman to achieve renown among men; self-assertion earns a woman an evil reputation.'[71] The Syrophoenician could not be assertive or devious in her reply but had to be the model woman and mother, symbolising the model church. According to the anonymous author of *Short Comments on Every Chapter of the Holy Bible*, 'As she was a good woman, so a good mother. This sent her to Christ.'[72] The heroism of the woman[73] lay in her grief and

---

68. CP Gilman, *The Man-made Word or Our Androcentric Culture* (New York: Charlton, 1911), 32.
69. M'Farlane, 49.
70. Even down to comparing, for example, the British Empire with the Roman Empire and adopting art styles, patterns of rhetoric that drew on ancient patterns. This materially bolstered one major philosophy of history: history was the servant of eternal verities because of the ability to point to longevity of practice! This had an added dimension, given England's imperial rule in India, which similarly drew on Roman parallels; see RS Sugirtharajah 'Imperial Critical Commentaries', in *Journal for the Study of the New Testament* 73 (1999): 103, and n45 above for an example.
71. SB Pomeroy, *Goddesses, Whores, Wives and Slaves: Women in Classical Antiquity* (New York: Schocken Books, 1975), 109.
72. *Short Comments on Every Chapter of the Holy Bible*, 59.
73. Olshausen calls her one of the 'heroes of the faith from amidst the heathen world' (203).

dependent faith, certainly not in her words. TT Lynch rejected anything positive in the woman's reply in these terms: 'Is there anything more than the ready tongue of woman, of whom it is said, "You shall never take her without her answer, unless you take her without her tongue?"'[74] Rather, in the Oxford-published words of Isaac Williams:

> We must observe of this suppliant, that she sees herself truly in the mirror of God's presence: she takes the position assigned to her by His sacred providence.[75]

Williams is completely oblivious that the text itself has become a mirror of his own (ideal) world. Here are combined the notions of providence, determinism, divine order, and a woman's authorised view of herself.

More liberal nineteenth century attitudes held her reply as singular, unrepeatable by most women, even though they were to imitate her faith and sorrow. Thus, JB Lightfoot, deemed that 'the famous heroines of womanhood will necessarily be few'. He went on, in this anniversary sermon for the *Girls' Friendly Society*,[76] that 'generally it is in the quieter, less obtrusive, more homely, and more womanly way, that she is called to test her power, certainly not less real or less beneficent, though it may be less striking, than the power of man. She is a mother in her own household . . . .' All this was delivered by the Bishop of Durham from the pulpit of St. Paul's Cathedral in London, symbolically and silently conveying the boundaries of the Church's tolerance, even in beneficent mode. By contrast, in American, the Quaker, Lucretia Mott, argued against 'the priestcraft and monopoly of the pulpit which have so long held women bound.'[77]

---

74. Quoted in a collection of interpreters' comments on the story in *The Expository Times* 4 (1892-3): 81.
75. Williams, 28.
76. JB Lightfoot, 'Woman and the Gospel' (preached June 19th 1884) in *Sermons* (The Contemporary Pulpit Library) (London: Swan Sonnenschein & Co, 2nd edition, 1892), 116-28.
77. D Greene (editor), *Lucretia Mott: Her Complete Speeches and Sermons* (New York / Toronto: Edwin Mellen Press, 1980), 28. She knew also the sway that was exercised: 'Women in particular have pinned their faith to ministers' sleeves. They dare not rely on their own God-given powers of discernment.' (Sermon at Yardleyville, Pennsylvania, 1858, printed in Hallowell 514.)

Humble Faith not Assertive Word wins Heroic Status

The opponent of this exemplary feminine faith was 'explanations or descriptions'.[78] The faith of (in) motherhood and household was eminently to be preferred to learning. Consequently, *for women* faith dominated word. The very element that might authorise women's claims upon education (as the industry of the word, as the industry under the control of men) was thereby eliminated,[79] even as the Markan Jesus' second response was marginalised. James Wells expressly castigated his present day: 'It is an interesting fact that, so far as we know, no woman ever opposed Christ in the days of His flesh. Some graceless women oppose Him in our day in public lectures; but this is a new horror, and a modern monstrosity.'[80]

Faith as the Solution to the Problems of History

There was a conceptual dimension to this accent on faith. Debates over history and dogma held faith to be the coveted spoils, frequently set against learning given that learning had become destructive of faith.[81] The Syrophoenician woman, slung with the sash of the 'ideal Church',[82] be-

---

78. Olshausen, 203.
79. By the turn of the twentieth century Adolf von Harnack and Willhelm Hermann were expressing extensive support for the education of women and in terms which included women's 'independence'; see *The Social Gospel* translated by GM Craik (London: Williams & Norgate, 1907), 116-21. Nevertheless, the primary though not sole aim of women's education must be marriage and the care of a family (130). Women working for educational opportunities, did not share such narrow visions. See Lucretia Mott's sermon at Bristol, Pennsylvania in 1860 printed in Hallowell, 527. By 1900, the views of FD Maurice (himself a promoter in the 1850s of the style of women's education Harnack and Hermann supported) that women's health would be adversely affected if they were admitted to, say, mathematics, were being dismissed by women educators as 'quaint'. (Gadesden, 87). On nineteenth century arguments that women were not able to enjoy the same education because it would damage their biological function, see Janet Sayers, *Biological Politics: Feminist and Anti-Feminist Perspectives* (London/New York: Tavistock Publications, 1982), 7-10.
80. J Wells, *Bible Children: Studies for the Young* (London: James Nisbet, 1879), 216-7.
81. There was perhaps some substance in the concern. The publication of *Essays and Reviews* in England (1860) either prompted or gave permission to many educated lay people, such as Lord and Lady Amberley (John Russell and Catherine (née) Stanley) to dispense with traditional frameworks of Christian faith: B and P Russell, *The Amberley Papers: The Letters and Diaries of Lord and Lady Amberley* (London: Hogarth Press, 1937), Volume 1, 258.
82. The Syrophoenician thereby became concurrently the image of the ideal woman and also the image of the ideal church, both struck by male theologians and Scriptural

came the lay hero of that faith required to withstand the destabilisation coming from male fields of learning.[83] Scholarship was rendered unnecessary, as also the fight for access. Here was a powerful political reason for preserving the Matthean rendition over the Markan.

The Syrophoenician Woman as Foil to Jesus' Masculinity

The affirmation of the woman as mother did not provide any individuation for her but rather served two functions. She acted primarily as a foil for Jesus and as such was divested of any distinctive gendered significance. That the immediate parallel to the story—the Centurion and his servant—was often noted, had the consequence of crafting the salient features of the Syrophoenician's story in male terms,[84] even to her detriment.[85] 'Her faith was quickened by what she saw of Jesus.'[86] In this sense, the woman's role was turned to a self-effacing silhouette that highlighted and expanded the prominence of the man (both as protector and recipient).

Here the socio-political values, training and expectations in nineteenth century Euro/Anglo-centred culture were promenaded. When the woman received additional attention, it was secondary and in terms of an exposition of the exemplary female virtues of the age—faith, humility, prayerfulness—those virtues in fact which could best display the wisdom, astuteness and responsibility of the *paterfamilias*. The lines of the English

---

    commentators on behalf of a church whose structures were controlled by men. The problems of interpretation that a collation of the image of woman with a church controlled by males brings, demanded that this aspect be muted, but it was a fissure that widened in subsequent investigations.

83. *Short Comments on Every Chapter of the Holy Bible*, 59. Catherine Vaughan, the wife of the Rev'd Dr Charles Vaughan, headmaster at Harrow and later Master of the Temple and Dean of Llandaff, wrote to her cousin Louisa Stanley singling out Jowett for criticism with regard to *Essays & Reviews* (Mar 2, 1863). When *Ecce Homo* was published anonymously she commented again on the connection between the two: '. . . yes, I have just read "Ecce Homo" and think it only a shade less offensive than Rénan. It is a Unitarian book—taking only a human view of our Lord and I think it often speaks of him and of his work in very irreverent terms . . . and then the "Lord's Supper" being compared to a "Club Dinner" is I do think too outrageous . . . I wonder who wrote it? I would almost fancy Jowett.' (Jan 31 [1865?]) (Cheshire Record Office: DSA 135).

84. Cowan, 693; Lindsay, 270.

85. Thus Weiss held that the Centurion's great faith was readily apparent, the woman's not so, requiring Jesus to test whether 'the like conditions obtained here.' (*Life*, 3.38).

86. Gould, *Mark*, 137.

poet laureate, Alfred Tennyson, in the enormously popular *The Princess* (1847) both expressed and cultivated such sensibilities:

> Man with the head, and woman with the heart
> Man to command, and woman to obey
> All else confusion.[87]

The Syrophoenician's acceptance of Jesus' argument had to be 'Yes' (7:28) and ναί vigorously held its position in the critical Greek editions of the New Testament produced in the course of the century:[88]

> She acknowledges the justice of our Saviour's observation. She concedes the principle of action that was implied.... [But] it would not be inconsistent with the prerogatives of the Jews, that a poor Gentile in her position should get the

---

87. The actual influence of this poem ought not be consigned merely to the realms of ideology. The future Archbishop of Canterbury and close friend of the famous Cambridge biblical triumvirate, himself the author of an acclaimed text on Cyprian, laid hold of Tennyson's poem as the warrant for his proposal to his future wife, Mary Sidgwick, then 11 years old. EW Benson was aged twenty-three at the time of avowing his adoration through the words of 'The Princess' which the young Mary had been reading: see A Benson, *As We Were: A Victorian Peep-Show* (London: Longmans, Green & Co, 1926), 60. Only after the dutiful filial biography of Benson (published 1899), did Arthur Benson discover his mother's deep fear of his father, consequent perhaps on her having 'set herself to man' (a line from 'The Princess' used by Arthur Benson to describe his mother's commitment [64]).
88. Ναί itself was probably an early intrusion of the text of Matthew (15:27) upon Mark under a combination of both assimilating tendencies and the desire to supply a fitting decorum of humility and acceptance to the woman. (See WD Davies and DC Allison, *The Gospel According to St. Matthew* (ICC) (Edinburgh: T&T Clark, 1991) Volume 2, 555.) Only Westcott and Hort allowed the possibility that ναί was to be omitted by marking its absence as a marginal alternative in their 'List of Noteworthy Rejected Readings'. Richard Weymouth recorded this as WHm in his *The Resultant Greek Testament* (London: Marshall Brothers, 1896), 109. However, it was not enough to persuade the whole committee working on the English Revised Version even to consider it. It was the force of P[45] that swung the ναί *out of* the critical text. Bruce Metzger applies internal considerations (the absence of ναί in Mark's Gospel compared with its frequency in Matthew, plus the power of assimilation) to explain its presence in the majority of manuscripts: *A Textual Commentary on the Greek New Testament* (UBS, 1971), 95. Even though absent from the critical Greek text, the hold of this acceding interpretation remains: see C Waetjen, *A Reordering of Power: A Socio-Political Reading of Mark's Gospel* (Minneapolis: Augsburg, 1989), 135, TE Boomershine, *Story Journey: An Invitation to the Gospel as Storytelling* (Nashville: Abingdon, 1988), 108, 109.

advantage of the little superfluity of ministerial or mediatorial help that was ready to drop . . .[89]

One can detect in the background here, the nineteenth century ecclesial understanding of charity for the desolate.[90] Hence FJA Hort, another Cambridge Professor, described it as the granting of a boon, which did not contravene the established and dutiful arrangement.[91]

The Sacrifice of Woman's Body and Mind to the Soul

There was a more sinister dimension to this emphasis on 'little'. Sarah Grimké's criticism of the limitations on women's education in the early nineteenth century, tellingly observed that the restriction was connected with the reiteration of women's maternal provision of food.[92] This obligation carried with it a notion of sacrifice—the self-denial of both education *and* appetite:

> A delicate appetite was much preferred and young women might be forced to nibble scraps in their bedroom so they might face the dinner table with ladylike anorexia.[93]

Although there is no explicit equation made in commentary, the constant emphasis on crumbs (7:28, Matt 15:27), and an acceptance of absence from the table ('in their bedroom') resonates with the recommended etiquette for women. 'Transcendent feminine modesty' required that ethereal spiritual aspirations be symbolised through bodily immateriality and subjection of sexuality. Any somatic subjectivity was expunged. The female body was written into anorexic, pre-Raphaelite submission.[94] Thus,

---

89. Morison, 212-3.
90. There was a double-sided appeal: the beneficent church mirrored Jesus and needy simple believers mirrored the Syrophoenician woman.
91. FJA Hort, *Judaistic Christianity* (edited by JOF Murray) (Grand Rapids, Mich: Baker Book House 1980 [1896]), 34-5.
92. SM Grimké, *Letters on the Equality of the Sexes and the Condition of Women* (New York: Burt Franklin, 1970 [1838]), Letter 8.
93. C Willett Cunnington, *Feminine Attitudes in the Nineteenth Century* (London: William Heinemann, 1935), 84.
94. See generally Michie, *Flesh Made Word*.

part of the civilising integral to the christianising of the heathen woman, was to allow her but 'small inconsiderable crumbs'.[95]

The dangerous sexual creature lurks in the background of this interest in food.[96] Jesus becomes the fitting object for the receipt of desire and the means by which such desire is sublimated, especially as fed by crumbs: 'Her faith and humility are more and more inflamed and stimulated by the repulse she met with in the first instance.'[97] Here the centurion comparisons depart, no such sexually charged innuendo being permitted to contaminate the story of a male Gentile's faith. Gendered pressures were mounting in nineteenth century society—a (re)problematisaton of woman, in and from the story, had begun.[98]

The Protection of Male Prerogative in Learning

'... how great was the terror of learned ladies' was a comment made by one school mistress of mid-nineteenth century England about the education of women.[99] Jesus being won over by the woman's ingenious argument was rarely noted.[100] Rather, the Syrophoenician's reply was characterised as an acceptance of Jesus' prioritising the Jews, or as the pitiable persistence of the needy distraught mother, or as a praiseworthy demonstration of a faithful extension of a hint that Jesus had hidden in his ruling. Jesus was the educated educator; the woman, at best, the emaciated mimetic.

The natural order declared that certain privileged men were the speakers of such language as expressed important ideas. In the nineteenth century European world, such a relative weighting was reflected in the denial of women's access to universities.[101] Publishing adopted similar carefully

---

95. Morison, 212-213.
96. Michie, *Flesh Made Word*, 15.
97. MacEvilly 283. It is striking that the Canaanite/Syrophoenician woman's story figured in the spiritualised eroticism of the divine bridal chamber in Christian gnosticism: see *Anonymous Apocrypha Gospel of Philip* 2 (Coptic Gospel of Philip), 122.109.21.
98. The suggestion that this was a re-problematisation is based on a reading of the earliest commentaries on the Syrophoenician / Canaanite / Hellenic woman, such as that by John Chrysostom.
99. One Miss Zimmern, quoted by Gadesden, 87.
100. The germ (but no more) of this interpretation is present in Erasmus *Commentary on Mark* (LB VII.212-3, Volume 49 of Erasmus *Collected Works* translated by E Rummel (Toronto: University of Toronto Press, 1988)).
101. Paris only opened its degree-doors to women in 1880, the first European university to do so. In England, the University of Durham broke the ceiling on the conferral of degrees to women in 1896.

protected boundaries. With most biblical commentators writing from positions in institutions that were denying or restricting the access of women, it is hardly likely that the Syrophoenician woman *would* be permitted to be a prototypical learned lady! Moreover, the generic christian valorisation of faith over learning, could be deftly diverted to the denial of women's entry into the dangerous realms of education.[102] A number of biblical commentators sharply criticised women who refused to accept the judgements of those institutions, which resisted women's passage from traditional patterns:

> The woman's faith, however, humbly receives the reply in all its bitterness, and child-like she takes the position assigned her, claiming no place within the temple; she is content to remain standing as a door-keeper in the outer court, and pleads simply for that grace which was fitting for the occupant of such a station.[103]

The allusion to the Gentile court provides the warrant for the hierarchy (gender and class) of relationship. The intertextual reference to door-keeper (Ps 84:10; compare Jn 18:16) fixes the woman's place as on a par with the female servant in the courtyard, part of the paraphernalia of established traditional culture. Others would push her further out, with one commentator paraphrasing her in Chrysostom-like terms: "'It is true", she said, "O Lord! I am not thy child—I am a dog.'"[104]

The classical ethos dominated male education in the nineteenth century. It provided an arsenal of linguistic (and related) weapons of gender control, notably violence, desire, hierarchy, and guardianship. Jesus became the personification of the model for the moulding of a woman, especially since she needed training in the faith to be the (re-)formed exemplar of faith for others. Through fixture on Jesus, desire was corrected and the woman would achieve, according to Olshausen, that 'faith [which] is again obviously seen not as knowledge, not as the upholding of certain doctrines for true, but as an internal state of mind—the tenderest susceptibility for what is heavenly—the most entire womanhood of the soul.'[105]

---

102. Luckock, *Footprints*, 264.
103. Olshausen, 2.203; see also J Ford, *The Gospel of S. Matthew* (London: Joseph Masters, 2nd edition, 1889), 284, Luckock, *Footprints*, 261, 264.
104. Williams, 28; compare Horsley, *Sermons*, 168.
105. Olshausen, 2.203. The more historically-radical James Seeley in his *Ecce Homo* un-

Quite clearly the Syrophoenician woman had become a slate on which to inscribe prescriptions related to women and their aspirations in the nineteenth century. That men held the written, spoken (preached) and published word underscores the parallels between the classical world and a century aspiring to view itself as equal to or surpassing the achievements of that past. Women are to be like servants therefore—anonymous, subsuming their own background, yet always present to support and assist, ignorant yet faithful.[106] The crossing of the boundaries such as would carve the woman her own identity was as abhorrent as a servant crossing the boundary to become a gentleman's wife.[107]

Women Reading the Syrophoenician

The contemporary writings of women do betray a substantial dependence on male scholarship, to which, at best, they could gain but restricted access,[108] even as they were required to submit to it.[109] Mabel Lindsay disavowed any attempt to make an academic contribution, and dutifully recorded her dependence on a male patron.[110] Her treatment of the story of the Syrophoenician woman explicitly names Alfred Edersheim as the source of the notion that Jesus did not enter into Gentile territory.

She retains the anti-semitism of inherited scholarship ('the fanatical Jews'), both of which (anti-Semitism and inherited scholarship) are sometimes deemed a problem in christian feminist writings.[111] And she endorses the hierarchy of relationship marked in Jesus' response to the

---

selfconsciously operated with the stereotyped triad of policing-whorish-reformed woman (248-50).
106. See B Robbins, *The Servant's Hand: English Fiction from Below* (Durham/London: Duke University Press, 1986).
107. B Hill, *Servants: English Domestics In The Eighteenth Century* (Oxford: Clarendon Press, 1996), 210.
108. Girton College, set up in Cambridge to provide degree level education for women, lists one person (name unknown) as having passed exams for theology. However, degrees were not awarded for the achievement at Cambridge until well into the twentieth century.
109. Women's writing was substantially circumscribed to repetition of men's work for the young and semi-literate. See RM Kachur, 'Envisioning Equality, Asserting Authority: Women's Devotional Writings on the Apocalypse, 1845-1900', in Melnyk, 4.
110. Lindsay, *Anni Domini*, Preface.
111. Schüssler Fiorenza, *Jesus*, 67-73.

woman: 'In her humility, she willingly accepted the inferior position'.[112] However, she reserved for her conclusion a guarded hint of the gendered dimensions of the story and the failure of scholarship and the Church to give them their due:

> ... nigh two thousand years have passed since the sound of His voice was heard, saying, 'O woman, great is thy faith: be it unto thee even as thou wilt'.[113]

The very existence of her writing provides a material witness to the effort for that voice to be heard.

Elizabeth Cady Stanton stands more squarely on her own authority in her treatment of the story. The collection, *The Woman's Bible*, which she edited, sought to isolate those biblical texts about women along with those texts that appear deliberately to have excluded women.[114] The story of the Syrophoenician woman is included precisely because of its gendered dimensions. There is a certain reticence in adopting the advice of commentators, though she harmonises Mark's account to that of Matthew. Nevertheless, Stanton acclaims that the woman 'proved herself quite equal in argument with Jesus', making 'her points ... with remarkable clearness'. The main obduracy however was not Jesus but his disciples (a model of the male-structured Church?) though she describes Jesus' saying as 'very ungracious'.

The importance of these voices, and other women's voices that have been noted herein, is that the appearance of the naturalness of male description and prescription is exposed as just that—an apparition.

Conclusion

The lines of interpretation of the Syrophoenician's story in the early period of modern critical scholarship were these: the historical and confessed Jesus, the relationship between Matthew's story of the Canaanite woman and Mark's Syrophoenician, the intent of the words Jesus addresses to the

---

112. Lindsay, 270.
113. Lindsay, 271.
114. EC Stanton (editor), *The Woman's Bible* (Salem, NH: Ayer Co, 1895 [reprinted 1986]), 5.

woman in the first instance in the story, the function of women in society and church, issues of mission, and to a lesser extent, race.

With the hindsight of historical perspective, one can identify the cultural and ideological commitments of interpreters, who were sometimes barely aware of how their critical presentation was being influenced by their socio-cultural location.[115] The push of women for equity of access to education attracted a specific temporal application of the traditional accent on the Syrophoenician woman's faith over her knowledge. Other related accents were aligned with this resistance through biblical commentary—domesticity, model motherhood, sanctified etiquette. The Syrophoenician became obedient to the response of the man Jesus and his hints that invited persistence within permitted bounds. Occasionally there were suggestions of women's own wayward sexual proclivities that required the straightening focus upon / of the Holy One.

The utilisation of the story to maintain idealised stabilities of relationships and functions within society was bolstered also by the portrayal of Jesus as an exemplary nineteenth century *paterfamilias* and manly citizen. Jesus remained quietly and determinedly loyal to the path that had been prescribed for him by the highest authority. This exemplary path was reinforced by the woman's humble acceptance of it. She, as a figure of foreign nations, provided the expected laudatory response and a warrant for contemporary missiological activity in Europe's trading posts.

Martin Kähler perceived at the time that the historical Jesus simply delivered a 'modern example of human creativity . . . the image of Jesus is being refracted through the spirit of these gentlemen themselves.'[116] This sweeping survey has revealed that, whether committed to historical or traditionalist approaches, the dominant lines of interpretation were forged in the mould of nineteenth century concerns about race (including anti-semitism), gender, class with its charity dimensions, trade, mission, faith, history and education.

And in general terms the passage became the means by which the larger philosophical debates about word and faith, language, history and ideas could be conducted and tested. Such debates, as rarefied as they sometimes were, nevertheless were intertwined with political tensions and struggles firmly planted in the nineteenth century context.

---

115. See BK Blount, *Cultural Interpretation: Reorienting New Testament Criticism* (Minneapolis: Fortress Press, 1995).
116. Kähler 43, 57 (compare also 55–6).

The survey has concentrated largely on one venue of interpretation—male-controlled academia and publishing. These have been handled critically and set against a modicum of recovered alternate assessments, thereby establishing the potential for multiple readings to unfold. But this conjunction has also highlighted the usually-undisclosed interests of many writers in the maintenance of the privileges of their position and profession through the passage being interpreted. The sheer concentration of those who interpreted the story is itself a commentary—few women interpreters lie in the inheritance of interpretation of this passage in the nineteenth century.[117] Commentary is located in official church and academic circles, most usually in combination. Like Hermes, the dog-throttler, they silenced the disruptive animal.

Certain aspects of the story and its interpretation were found to be muted. A few socio-cultural dimensions were added for colour and to satisfy a developing nineteenth century European market for 'Eastern' curios, but little more. Only because of the apologetic concern about the thrust of 'dogs' in Jesus' words was a little more enquiry made. But even here the prompting apologetic concern yielded a dominant apologetic result.

Those aspects of the story that pertain to the healing of the possessed daughter are notable for their absence or insignificant treatment. The woman was hard enough to contain in the interpretation of the story; a daughter was nigh impossible.

The concerns that found a convenient canvas for expression in the Syrophoenician story have substantially framed the interpretation of this pericope throughout the twentieth century. The import of the story was resolutely harnessed to the word. This 'logocentricity'[118] organised centre and periphery. Even when emphases changed in the following century, the hold of the word remained virtually unquestioned. Catherine Elsmere, a

---

117. For all that, nineteenth century feminist preachers and writers like Lucretia Mott, Ellice Hopkins, Sarah Grimké, Mary Wollstonecraft and others did exploit the contributions of biblical figures such as Phoebe, Prisca, and the Samaritan woman familiar in feminist interpretation today, the Syrophoenician woman is rarely mentioned. This remains a puzzle, though one might speculate at her expropriation by male churchmen and theologians to be the exemplar of their own commitments and prescriptions.

118. 'Logocentricity' seems to be a neologism of deconstructionist theory, which has passed into widespread usage. It connotes the privileged position given to speech and writing. When found in feminist theory it is sometimes combined with 'phallocentrism' to indicate the connection between speech and text, and the male interests both are made to serve. See M Coleridge, 'In Defence of the Other: Deconstruction and the Bible' in *Pacifica* 5 (1992): 130.

character in Mary Ward's late-nineteenth century novel, raised one woman's protest against the period's theological struggles. A century further on, they still await exploration: 'Words are nothing.'[119]

---

119. M Ward, *Robert Elsmere* (London: Macmillan & Co, 1888), 530.

Chapter Nine
Imposing the Silence of Women:
A Suggestion about the Date of the Interpolation in 1 Corinthians

Shelly Li

This essay accepts that the verses in 1 Corinthians 14 that state that 'women should be silent in the churches' (v 34f) most likely did not come from Paul's hand.[1] The First Letter of Clement to the Corinthians can provide us with some clues as to when the interpolation has entered the text. This study will give us a glimpse of how Paul was interpreted in a text written between thirty and fifty years after Paul wrote the Corinthian letters.[2] Clement seems to have been familiar with Paul's letters to the Corinthians and it appears that 1 Corinthians has influenced the writing of 1 Clement. Yet the writer of 1 Clement does not appear to impose the same constraints upon women as is found in the Corinthians muzzling passage. Rather he endorsed Rahab and her prophetic gift and called her a woman of faith in parallel to Abraham the father of faith. This essay argues that this explicit support for Rahab's prophecy shows that Clement probably had not seen the passage in 1 Corinthians 14 which states that women should keep silence and be submissive.

---

1. An extended defence of this position from a Singaporean, feminist perspective, is found in my unpublished doctoral thesis, 'Women (No Longer) Keep Silent: A Singaporean, Chinese, Pentecostal, Feminist Reading of 1 Cor 14:34–35' PhD Thesis, Flinders University, 2007.
2. David Horrell surveys a range of options proposed since the seminal work of JB Lightfoot (*The Apostolic Fathers. Part I: S. Clement of Rome. A Revised Text with Introductions, Notes, Dissertations and Translations*, Volume 1 [London and New York: Macmillan, 1890]) and comes out in agreement with him (95–96 CE). See his *The Social Ethos of the Corinthian Correspondence* (Edinburgh: T&T Clark, 1996), 239.

Introduction to 1 Clement

1 Clement is one of the earliest Christian writing outside the New Testament. Originating from Rome, the letter gives us glimpses of the circumstances and attitudes of Roman Christians, which appear quite different from those of some Christians in Asia Minor evidenced in Revelation. The Roman government, for example, appears in a more positive light (1 Clem 60:4 – 61:3) and extols conventional Roman values, such as peace, harmony, and order.

The text known as 1 Clement is, from its own internal evidence, a letter sent from the church at Rome to the church at Corinth. Although 1 Clement was not included in the final New Testament Canon, it was, and is, an important and influential document, being addressed to the same community to which Paul wrote. 1 Corinthians has influenced the writing of 1 Clement; however, Pauline materials are beginning to be interpreted in 1 Clement in a new light, now thirty to fifty years after Paul wrote. Although Clement did draw on Paul's ideas, he began to utilise Pauline materials in his own context. Though the same words or phrases as deployed by Paul may be used, their meanings are often different in 1 Clement. Clement applied his own hermeneutics to the thoughts and materials that have originated from a Pauline background.

An Overview of the Problem at Corinth[3]

Right at the start of the letter, Clement singled out the problem the church is experiencing. The Roman's church has been alerted and is now concerned about a dispute at Corinth. There has been 'abominable and unholy sedition' (μιαρᾶς καὶ ἀνοσίου στάσεως) caused by 'a few rash and self-willed people' (1:1).[4] It is clear that Clement wants to restore peace and harmony within the church and his concern about this 'sedition' (στά σις) is evident throughout the letter.[5] As a whole, Clement's letter very much looks like an 'entreaty for peace and concord' (63:2).[6] 1 Clem 47:6

---

3. For this section I am especially indebted to JS Jeffers, *Conflict at Rome: Social Order and Hierarchy in Early Christianity* (Minneapolis: Fortress Press, 1991).
4. The text of 1 Clement is taken from Kirsopp Lake (editor and translator), *Apostolic Fathers* (Loeb Classical Library) (London: William Heinemann Ltd, 1977). Translations are adapted from his.
5. Note the frequent use of στασιάζω (4:12; 43:2; 46:7; 47:6; 49:5; 51:3; 55:1), στάσις (1:1; 2:6; 3:2; 14:2; 46:9; 51:1; 54:2; 57:1; 63:1).
6. Note εἰρηνεύω (15:1, 54:2, 56:12f; 63:4), εἰρήνη (2:2; 3:4; 15:1; 16:5; 19:2; 20:1, 9ff;

doubtlessly tells us the nature of the στάσις: the Corinthian church has been led 'through one or two people to rebel against the elders'. It has become particularly fraught because the appointed elders have been removed from their positions (44:3–6).

The disunity that the church experienced during Paul's time appears now still to be continuing or is happening all over again. This time the disruption is caused by house church rivalry and inter-household strife. The letter suggests that the 'trouble-makers' are those from a lower social position. These people 'from below' are rebelling and leading others to rebel against household heads, that is, the 'elders'.

Just like Paul in 1 Corinthians, Clement is disturbed by the lack of peace and the disorder in the church community. In 1 Corinthians, Paul condemns 'division' and 'dissension' in the congregation (1 Cor 1:10; 11:18; 12:25). He emphasises that God's way in all the churches is 'one of peace and not disorder' (1 Cor 14:33). To Paul, everything must be done in a non-chaotic and orderly way in worship (1 Cor 14:40).

Clement is taking up and dealing with Pauline concerns again.[7] He explicitly mentions Paul in chapter 47 and makes reference to his attempt to confront division in the church just as he himself is doing. Both Paul and Clement express a concern for unity and harmony in the congregation. However, the situations are different.

In 1 Corinthians, Paul is addressing problems that involve inter personal conflicts and ethical issues. Some members in the congregation do not see eye to eye with one another; some are claiming spiritual superiority over the other members, and trying to achieve it through ecstatic acts during the course of their worship services. The ecstatic members of the community would prophesy and make proclamations in languages unknown to people. They try to surpass one another by manifesting their abilities to speak in tongues. They show this one-upmanship not only in the worship service; some were even bold enough to take others whom they disagreed with to court. In addition, 'the personal conduct of community members was not at all what Paul had in mind when he led them away from what he viewed as their degenerate pasts into the church of Christ.'[8] At their agape pre-communion meals, some would gorge them-

---

21:1; 22:5; 60:3f; 61:1f; 62:2; 63:2; 64:1; 65:1), ὁμόνοια (9:4; 11:2; 20:3, 10f; 21:1; 30:3; 34:7; 49:5; 50:5; 60:4; 61:1; 62:2 [ὁμονοέω]; 63:2; 65:1).

7. Horrell, *Social Ethos*, 253.
8. Gerd Theissen, *The Social Setting of Pauline Christianity*, edited and translated by J Schütz (Philadelphia: Fortress Press, 1982), 179.

selves and get drunk while others would come late and find nothing to eat. Some of the men in the congregation visited prostitutes and did not think that it was wrong (1 Cor 6:15–20); one of the men was even sleeping with his stepmother (1 Cor 5:1). This was basically the community that Paul addressed.[9] Clement, on the other hand, was chiefly concerned about the social strife of a few from the 'lower class' (that is, lower in social position and status) rising against the leadership in the church.[10]

Clement repeatedly drew upon the Scriptures to demonstrate that the problems of sinners have always been envy and strife, wrought in opposition to the righteous. Clement cites Old Testament examples of jealousy and rivalry running from Cain and Abel to his own day, injected into the text in an effort to restore a sense of discipline to the Corinthian 'usurpers'. He also used the words of the prophets to show that God is against those who exalt themselves over the ones whom he has chosen. He also applied the teachings of Jesus and then he specifically cited Paul (1 Clem 47:1–3) before directing the citation to his plea (1 Clem 48:1).

> Take up the epistle of the blessed Paul the Apostle. What did he first write to you at the beginning of his preaching? With true inspiration he charged you concerning himself and Cephas and Apollos . . . Let us then quickly put an end to this, and let us fall down before the Master, and beseech him with tears that he may have mercy upon us, and be reconciled to us, and restore us to our holy and seemly practice of love for the brothers and sisters.

Clement urged the Corinthians to reflect upon the epistle of Paul and consider his teaching that all belongs to Christ, that there should not be factions aligned with himself or Cephas or Apollos. Likewise, the Corinthians should end their rivalry and strife in the congregation. Here we are on the way to having uniquely Christian authorities serve as the ultimate arbiter over matters of faith and practice.

In 1 Clement 37:5 – 38:2, Clement uses the Pauline metaphor of the body to describe the natural interdependence the congregation should have as a Christian body.

---

9. Ibid.
10. Horrell, *Social Ethos*, 249.

Let us take our body; the head is nothing without the feet, likewise the feet are nothing without the head; the smallest members of our body are necessary and valuable to the whole body, but all work together and are united in a common subjection to preserve the whole body.

Let, therefore, our whole body be preserved in Christ Jesus, and let each be subject to his neighbour, according to the position granted to him. Let the strong care for the weak and let the weak reverence the strong. Let the rich man bestow help on the poor and let the poor give thanks to God, that he gave him one to supply his needs; let the wise manifest his wisdom not in words but in good deeds; let him who is humble-minded not testify to his own humility, but let him leave it to others to bear him witness; let not him who is pure in the flesh be boastful, knowing that it is another who bestows on him his continence.

Each member of the body is essential for the well-being of the whole; no one is more important than the other. All members should work together as a whole. Likewise, members in the congregation should subject themselves to one another, each caring for one another. Clement's use of the metaphor of the body starkly resembles the language and concept of Paul in 1 Cor 12:

As it is, there are many parts, yet one body. The eye cannot say to the hand, 'I have no need of you,' nor again the head to he feet, 'I have no need of you.' On the contrary, the parts of the body which seem to be weaker are indispensable, and those parts of the body which we think less honourable we invest with the greater honour, and our unpresentable parts are treated with greater modesty, which our more presentable parts do not require. But God has so composed the body, giving the greater honour to the inferior part, that there may be no discord in the body, but that the members may have the same care for one another.

Both Paul and Clement say that the head cannot do without the feet, and vice versa. Even the 'smallest' (Clement's terminology: ἐλάχιστα μέλη) or the 'weaker' (Paul's terminology: ἀσθενέστερα) parts or members of our body are also indispensable. Clement goes on to point out that the strong in the church should care for the weak and the rich ones should help the poor. He reaffirmed the idea that members should not claim superior status in the body, whether based on social position or, more important for Clement's argument, on 'spiritual gifts'.

For Clement, order and submission are essential for the proper functioning of the congregation, and for the preservation (σώζεσθαι) of the whole body. He despised the schism and discord in Corinth and hoped that members would respond with a yearning for communal cohesion. Clement's primary aim was to restore proper order within the Corinthian church; to re-establish the position of the deposed presbyters and to end the στάσις." Considering this purpose, we can see why Clement's rhetoric is more socially conservative than Paul's. To Clement, the removal of the presbyters is a serious offense against the established order and practice of the community. To a greater degree, he supported the official, institutionalised roles in the community. Clement thus developed a theology of 'order' to a much greater extent than Paul. Winsome Munro sees in this the 'subjectionist' theme that characterises the 'Pastoral Stratum' that, clearly expressed in the Pastoral Letters, provides the overarching editorial principle shaping the Pauline corpus.[12] As we shall see, there are significant elements that suggest that 1 Clement pre-dates this Pastoral Stratum even if it may be on the trajectory leading to it.

The Roman Empire continued to develop its ideology and military prowess while keeping a tight control on its people. Despite the non-conducive climate, the Corinthian church bloomed quietly in the background. The legitimacy of Christianity was not recognised by the rulers but they were willing to close an eye as long as Christians did not make any trouble. 'Clement saw in the Corinthian uproar a threat to the tenuous peace with the State. Any insurrection within the church could cause a repeat of the Neronian persecution.'[13] Clement did not want any disturbance to attract the attention of the State, so there was more to his concern about strife than simply the inner life of the Christian community.

Clement asserted that dissension and schism had disturbed the peace of the Christian community. Christians had succumbed to their own selfish desires and were not living out their citizenship in a civil manner (3:4).

---

11. Francis Firth, 'The Letter of Clement of Rome', in the *Coptic Church Review* 6 (Nov 1988): 393–395.
12. See W Munro, *Authority in Paul and Peter: The Identification of a Pastoral Stratum in the Pauline Corpus and 1 Peter* (Cambridge: Cambridge University Press, 1983), 120.
13. Jeffers, *Conflict At Rome,* 96.

Those who 'live without regret as citizens of God' would leave and go away from the community rather than cause strife (54:4). Similarly, those who live in the 'fear and love' of God are willing even to suffer torture (51:2). Christians who perform good and virtuous deeds in harmony (ὁμόνοια) are acting as citizens worthy of God (21:1). One can clearly see here that Clement patterned congregational membership after citizenship in the Roman state. The society at that time largely respected Roman citizenship. 1 Clement adopted this view into Christianity. Clement's view of the church's organisation, therefore, has shifted from Paul's view, which had been more of a horizontal egalitarianism to one that was more hierarchical and vertical.

According to Clement, the proper role of Christians was to support peace, not to contest or upset it. He believed that, just as Rome remains in peace because all obey the emperor, the Christian community will remain in peace when all obey God, the Master, by remaining in submission to the congregation's leaders. Clement was familiar with Paul's teachings about the unity of the body of believers and the impropriety of dissension. But *Paul has been interpreted into Clement's context*. Clement has drawn upon Paul to create the idea that God, as Master of the Christians, is due as much obedience as the emperor receives from his subjects (50:4). The order which Clement sought to create within the church was that recommended by Roman political philosophy. Clement organised the congregation as a hierarchy, based on his positive view of Roman institutions. The hierarchical structure in 1 Clement eventually took root and became the format of the Roman church.[14]

Clement's notions of citizenship and civil harmony were also adopted from the Roman thinking. He considered 'the Roman army, the emperor's principal instrument for maintaining the Pax Romana, Peace of Rome, a fitting model for discipline and obedience in the church.'[15] Paying tribute to the army, he says (37:2–3):

> Let us consider those who serve our generals, with what good order, habitual readiness, and submissiveness they perform their commands. Not all are prefects, nor tribunes, nor centurions, nor in charge of fifty men, or the like, but each carries out in his own unit the commands of the emperor and of the generals.

---

14. Barbara Ellen Bowe, *A Church In Crisis* (Minneapolis: Fortress Press, 1988), 98.
15. Jeffers, *Conflict At Rome*, 139.

By proposing a more hierarchical church, Clement might have become the forerunner of the ideas of the later Pastoral Stratum. His thinking in 1 Clement might have prepared people for the introduction and application of the subjectionist passages of the Pastoral Stratum later on. With a Roman authority like Clement advocating a more vertical church structure, it would have made the later Pastoral Stratum more readily acceptable within the churches.

Another theme from Paul's letter to the Corinthians that is repeated in 1 Clement is 'love'. 1 Clement 49 is akin to a hymn of love resonating with 1 Corinthians 13. However, the only phrase identical between these two separate passages lies in ἀγάπη … πάντα μακροθυμεῖ (1 Clem 49:5 // 1 Cor. 13:4).[16] The term ἀγάπη is repeated even more in 1 Clement than in 1 Corinthians creating a persistent emphasis. Both Paul and Clement had adapted general praises of love to fit their respective purposes. Paul's concern in his interlude on Christian love in 1 Corinthians 13 is to redirect the Corinthians' thinking on the true nature of spirituality, and to re-direct their attention on tongues within the framework of the primacy of love in Christian ethics, so that their eagerness for 'spirits' will be turned toward edifying the community rather than given over to 'spirituality'. For Clement, 'love' is what the divisive church in Corinth is in need of. He believed that 'love', the over-arching virtue according to Paul, will overpower those vices which Clement considered were threatening to divide the church in Corinth in his own day. In love there is no haughtiness (ὑπερήφανος), no schism (σχίσμα), no sedition (στάσις); love does everything in concord (ὁμόνοια). Love is presented as the element necessary for preserving harmony among Christians. Clement also urged the church to beg and pray that members might be 'found in love', lead a peaceful community life, and be free from blame. To Clement, Christians perform the commandments of God in the concord of love; love shows itself in deeds performed in the harmony of love (ἐν ὁμονοίᾳ ἀγάπης, 50:5). Again, Clement has taken Pauline material and further developed it. He has emphasised the function of love in restoring peace and harmony within the church.

The Example of Rahab the Harlot

As we have seen, the discord and conflict apparent in the Corinthian Christian community addressed by Paul appear to be recurring among

---

16. Horrell, *The Social Ethos of the Corinthian Correspondence*, 253.

the descendants of that church near the end of the first century. The causes may be different but, again, the trouble has prompted the writing of a letter (1 Clem 47:7) and the sending of mediators, all with the avowed concern for the reputation of the Corinthian church (1:1) and a desire to reprimand and repair the behaviour (63:3, 65:1). Although the exact cause of the problem is unclear, it seems that some younger Christians in the assembly have grouped together to oppose their leaders (3:3; 44:6; 47:6). Peace, order, love and unity are emphasised as the values that are to characterise the life of the Church, operating within a proper structuring of and respect for the position of church members. This is the larger context within which 'a remarkable text'[17] occurs, a text that positively names Rahab the harlot.

From the comments attached to this biblical woman, we can gain a glimpse of how Clement viewed prophecy and a woman prophesying. He first praised her 'hospitality', perhaps more of a 'domestic' virtue, though similarly tied to her 'faith', a combination, as we shall see, that defies the notion that their attachment to Rahab is gender- and politically-specific. But he then commended to the sight of the Corinthian community, that there is 'not only faith, but also prophecy in this woman'. (12:8 ὅτι οὐ μόνον πίστις, ἀλλὰ καὶ προφητεία ἐν τῇ γυναικί). It is significant that Rahab was taken as a woman of both faith and prophecy here. This is where the date of the letter becomes significant, given the elapse of time from Paul's correspondence.

Rahab is not used as an isolated example (1 Clement 12) but is paralleled with Abraham (1 Clement 10) and Lot (1 Clement 11), perhaps also as a contrast from Lot's wife (1 Clem 11:2). It raises the issue of how such models would function for the membership and operations of the Corinthian community, a community that is riven by strife. These models are designed to provide biblical warrant for paradigms of imitation such as would counteract the divisive elements in the Corinthian community. These models are provided as cultivants and stimulants of the recommended behaviour.

Abraham is described as 'the friend (ὁ φίλος) ' (1 Clem 12:1), who was found faithful because he was obedient to the words of God. He obediently went out from his own country, and from his kindred, and from his father's house. By forsaking a small territory, a weak family, and an

---

17. The judgement of Margaret Y MacDonald, *Early Christian Women and Pagan Opinion: the power of the hysterical woman* (Cambridge: Cambridge University Press, 1996), 228.

insignificant house, he might inherit the promises of God, relying upon Genesis 12:1–3; 13: 14–16; 15:5–6. But of particular note is that because of his faith and hospitality, a son was given him in his old age. In obedience Abraham offered him as a sacrifice to God on one of the mountains which God showed him. All this outlines the picture of Abraham that Clement wishes to present. It culminates with the birth of Isaac which is grounded in the very same virtues that are used of Rahab: faith and hospitality.

Hospitality also characterises Lot, though this time, given Clement's propensity for parataxis, the pairing is with piety (εὐσέβεια). Such qualities are lacking in Lot's wife, whose prevarication and double-mindedness mark her for generations as the contrast.

Where one might have expected another woman to serve as a warning exemplar, Clement returned to a positive illustration. More than that, he elicits Rahab as an exemplar of the same virtues as found in Abraham. For Rahab, her faith and hospitality brings rescue (or 'salvation'—ἐσώθη). Clement unfolds the story of the hospitable Rahab, who received Joshua's spies and concealed them on the roof of her house under some stalks of flax. She protected them from the king's soldiers, recognising that the Lord God had given Jericho to Israel. The spies promised to protect her family, and they gave her a sign, a scarlet thread she should hang out of her house. Clement's interpretation of the story from Joshua pointedly makes Rahab (not Abraham) the one in whom Christian redemption 'through the blood of the Lord' (1 Clem 12.7) is proleptically to be found. It appears that both her avowal of faith and her action in the obedient display of the 'scarlet thread' as a 'foreshadowing' (πρόδηλον) of the future, attract the startling ascription of Rahab the prostitute as the bearer of prophecy. The woman is clearly not silent in either word or action and can be upheld as an exemplar for the proper operation of the Corinthian Christian community. Indeed in the four examples (three positive and one negative) in 1 Clement 10 to 12, only Rahab is specifically linked to the Christian dispensation.

There could be no greater contrast between two people than that which exists between Abraham and Rahab. Abraham is called by God to become the father of believers. Rahab is a Gentile, an inhabitant of ancient Jericho, destined for destruction by the Israelite army. As a man, Abraham is the representative head of God's covenant people. Rahab is a woman, known only as a prostitute. Abraham gave proof of his obedience to God for at least three decades. Rahab knew about Israel's God only by hearsay, yet she displayed her faith by identifying herself with God's people. It is thus significant that these two figures were placed side by side in 1 Clement and that Rahab is deemed prophetic and assumes the honour of being comparable to Abraham the father of faith.

Here then we find Clement's attitude towards women and prophecy at the end of the first century. And given the upholding of Rahab to view by the Corinthian community (ὁρᾶτε ἀγαπητοί) there is every expectation that the members of the community would find a correlation between their membership and the exemplary woman. For Clement, what 'Corinthian women prophets' there were,[18] were not to be silenced but to be wedded to their mother in prophecy, Rahab of Jericho, in her avowal of allegiance to the elect of God and in a faithful prophetic witness to Christian redemption.

If at this time Clement had read 1 Cor 14:34-35 as included in Paul's letter, it seems most unlikely that he would have written this. Not only did he endorse Rahab's faith and hospitality, he endorsed prophecy by a woman, the gift so highly valued by Paul (1 Cor 14:5). The Pauline Corinthian correspondence that Clement read was therefore most likely without verses 34-35 which gives the command that women are to keep silent and be submissive to their husbands. Accordingly, the insertion of verses 34-35 must have occurred after about 96 CE. Clement repeatedly quotes Paul in the letter (24:1; 34:8; 37:5 - 38:2; 41:1; 47; 49:5-6 as demonstrated) and clearly shows his familiarity with 1 Corinthians. Yet he did not pick up the elements in 1 Corinthians, as we have it now, that sought to silence women and may well have served a rhetorical purpose for his arguments about order, if he had known them.

Clement repeatedly quotes Paul but he does not touch on the issue of women's behaviour in the church, though the use of women to think with as a corrective of male and ecclesial behaviour would become writ large in the church in the near future. Either Clement has chosen to ignore the issue, or the subjectionist strain of the Pastoral Stratum was not present in the 1 Corinthians that was circulated at his time. However, his endorsing of Rahab's prophecy suggests that it is more probable that he has not seen any teaching (Pauline or 'Pastoral') requiring women not to teach or prophesy

---

18. Antoinette Wire sees Paul as using an appeal to law in 1 Cor 14:34 to silence (some of) Corinth's prophets: *The Corinthian Women Prophets: A Reconstruction through Paul's Rhetoric* (Minneapolis: Fortress Press, 1990), 20, 29. The argument here is that 1 Cor 14: 34-35 is actually post-Pauline and that 1 Clement, already on the trajectory to an ecclesial and familial patterning that is more conventional in societal terms, does not know of these verses as Pauline.

or speak in the church. Rather he identifies Rahab the woman prophet as providing a positive exemplar for the right behaviour and ordering of the church in Corinth, an exemplar that almost certainly was designed to elicit resonances amongst certain members of that church. Given that Clement was every-ready to draw on the pre-existing Pauline storehouse for both the characterisation of the ills in the Corinthian church and the diagnosis of remedies for those ills, he would have taken up the verses that ordered church life hierarchically if they had been present.

The Advent of the Pastoral Stratum

There has been consensus amongst scholars such as Raymond Brown, M.Dibelius, H Conzelmann, Raymond Collins and Luke Timothy Johnson that the Pastorals were written around 120 CE.[19] It is in the Pastoral Letters that we unequivocally find sentiments echoing that which we find in 1 Cor 14:34–35. Judging from our finding from 1 Clement, we can deduce that the interpolation of the Pastoral Stratum into Paul's letters across the board has taken place between 96 CE and 120 CE. This confirms the judgment made by Winsome Munro but modifies her suggestion that the Pastoral stratum began to find literary expression in the Pauline writings in Asia Minor and / or Rome from about 90 CE.[20] At least as regards the Pastoral stratum interpolation in 1 Corinthians 14, this must have found its way into the transmission of 1 Corinthians some time after Clement wrote to the Christian community in Corinth.

Conclusion

We have taken a glimpse of Clement's hermeneutical treatment of some Pauline materials. It is apparent that 1 Corinthians has influenced the writing of 1 Clement, although the Pauline materials were beginning to be interpreted in 1 Clement in new light 30 to 50 years later. The study suggests that Clement was familiar with 1 Corinthians; and yet he en-

---

19. Raymond Brown, *An Introduction*, 662; M Dibelius and H Conzelmann, *The Pastoral Epistles* (Philadelphia: Fortress Press, 1972), 178; Raymond F Collins, *1 & 2 Timothy and Titus: A Commentary* (Louisville, KY: Westminster/John Knox Press, 2002), 83; Luke Timothy Johnson, *Invitation to the New Testament Epistles III: A Commentary in Colossians, Ephesians, 1 Timothy, 2 Timothy, and Titus with Complete Text from the Jerusalem Bible* (Garden City, NY: Image Books, 1980), 378.
20. Munro, *Authority*, 134.

dorsed Rahab's prophecy. Clement was probably not familiar with the Pastoral Stratum that made its presence felt in the transmission of the Pauline Corpus, at least as regards 1 Corinthians. 1 Cor 14:34–35 therefore has entered the text after 1 Clement was written, sometime after 96 CE. The verses were probably interpolated early in the second century as part of a broader reworking of the Pauline letters that now generalised the subjectionist elements already visible in Colossians and Ephesians into a widespread Pastoral Stratum. Only after Clement would Rahab and her progeny be silenced.

Chapter Ten
Cohesion and Prominence in the Expository Discourse of Colossians

Philip McKeown

Introduction

Discourse Analysis is a relatively new approach to New Testament exegesis. It is an area of linguistics that is known by various names such as Text-linguistics, Text Analysis, Text Grammar and Discourse Studies.[1] Although there are numerous definitions, one of the most distinctive traits of Discourse Analysis is the view that the features of language should be understood and analysed at levels 'beyond the sentence'.[2] A simple definition of Discourse Analysis is the analysis of an entire text (a *discourse*) in relation to its *context*. Based on this understanding, some divide Discourse Analysis into the sub-fields of *text-linguistics* (analysis limited to the text) and *pragmatics* (analysis of extra-linguistic presuppositions).[3] This paper will focus on one particular feature of Discourse Analysis—the analysis of *cohesion* (how an author indicates to a reader that a text is unified, rather than just random words and sentences) and *prominence* (how an author indicates that certain ideas are more important than others).

---

1. JT Reed, *A Discourse Analysis of Philippians: Method and Rhetoric in the Debate over Literary Integrity* (Sheffield: Sheffield Academic Press, 1997), 18.
2. JP Louw, 'Discourse Analysis and the Greek New Testament', in *Bible Translator* 24/1 (1973): 101-118 at 103; JT Reed, 'Discourse Analysis', in *Handbook to Exegesis of the New Testament*, edited by Stanley E Porter (New York: Brill, 1997), 189-217 at 191; SH Levinsohn, *Discourse Features of New Testament Greek: A Coursebook on the Information Structure of New Testament Greek* (Dallas: Summer Institute of Linguistics, 2000), viii.
3. JB Green, 'Discourse Analysis and New Testament Interpretation', in *Hearing the New Testament: Strategies for Interpretation*, edited by Joel B Green (Grand Rapids: Eerdmans, 1995), 175-96 at 177.

The discourse that will be analysed is the first part of the epistle to the Colossians.

A criticism of Discourse Analysis has been that it is merely 'restating the obvious using unnecessarily forbidding terminology'.[4] This paper will show that the tools of Discourse Analysis, and particularly the features of *cohesion* and *prominence*, are useful for determining the main themes of a discourse and correctly identifying appropriate divisions within a discourse. It also has the potential to explain the function of some constituents that have otherwise remained debated. Where it does not provide an explanation, it does provide a precise meta-language which can be used to describe the analysis and evaluate competing interpretations. However, to maintain this precise meta-language, it is necessary to use technical terms throughout this paper. To reduce the 'forbidding' nature of these terms, this paper will briefly define and explain each term as it occurs.

The framework for Discourse Analysis used in this paper is Systemic-Functional Linguistics. Although Systemic-Functional Linguistics is not designed to be a method for Discourse Analysis, the advantage of this approach is that it gives a framework that relates the text to the context, as well as being general enough to be applied to various texts.[5] Before investigating the features of *cohesion* and *prominence*, it is helpful to understand where this concept fits within a Systemic-Functional Linguistics framework so that the limits of what it covers (and does not cover) can be clearly seen.

Overview of Systemic-Functional Linguistics

Text and Context

In Systemic-Functional Linguistics a *text* is any spoken or written passage, and is often contrasted with an unrelated collection of sentences.[6] It can be as short as one word (for example, 'Stop!') or as long as the longest work one can imagine. Although this definition allows for a wide range of communication to be described as *text*, 'the texts that yield the most consistent

---

4. Moisés Silva, 'Discourse Analysis and Philippians', in *Discourse Analysis and Other Topics in Biblical Greek* edited by Stanley E Porter and DA Carson (Sheffield: Sheffield Academic Press. 1995), 102-6 at 103.
5. Reed, *Philippians*, 61.
6. Michael AK Halliday and Ruqaiya Hassan, *Cohesion in English* (London: Longman, 1976), 1.

analysis are edited texts'.[7] These texts are 'the kind of discourses that other people want to listen to' because 'they are constructed according to plans that make it maximally easy for hearers or readers to comprehend them'.[8] The preservation and canonisation of the Biblical corpus is a result of the fact that people wanted to keep hearing these texts. The presupposition that the texts of the Bible have been inspired and appropriated by God also leads to the conclusion that the texts say what the author wants them to say and thus can be construed as 'edited texts'. In Systemic-Functional Linguistics the *context* is everything that surrounds the *text*. There are the three levels of *context*: Context of Culture, Context of Situation, and Co-text.

First, the *Context of Culture* is the assumed background knowledge behind the text.[9] There is the background of 'sociohistorical realities' and 'presupposition pools' that an author expects a model reader to have.[10] In Biblical studies this background knowledge is typically provided under the heading of 'New Testament Background'. There is also the knowledge of the language in which the text is written (for example, Koiné Greek), and the personal experience of each language user means that they will also develop their own unique variety of language which is known as their *idiolect*.[11]

Second, the *Context of Situation* is the environment in which the text occurs.[12] Information regarding the author, the recipients and their surroundings would be known to the original recipients. For example, the location of Colossae (Col 1:2), Paul's location when writing (4:9), the background events (1:4-8), and the teaching of Epaphras (1:7-8), would have been known to the Colossian recipients or could have been provided by Tychicus (4:9). These aspects are typically discussed in the Introduction to commentaries.[13] The interpretation of a text requires knowledge of these presuppositions which are shared by the author and audience.[14] However, this does not mean that the discourse is unintelligible without this back-

---

7. JE Grimes, *The Thread of Discourse* (The Hague: Mouton, 1975), 33.
8. Grimes, *Thread*, 33-4.
9. Michael AK Halliday and Ruqaiya Hassan, *Language, context, and text: Aspects of language in a social-semiotic perspective* (Melbourne: Deakin University Press 1985), 99.
10. Green, 'Discourse Analysis', 183, 185.
11. Reed, *Philippians*, 51-3.
12. Halliday and Hasan, *Language, context, and text*, 6.
13. Grimes, *Thread*, 19.
14. Reed, *Philippians*, 94.

ground knowledge because 'Text creates its own context'.[15] Aspects of the context can be reconstructed from the text because any 'piece of text, long or short, spoken or written, will carry with it indications of its context'.[16]

There is also a configuration of meanings that are typically associated with a particular situation.[17] When this configuration of meanings is expressed in a text it produces a *genre* which provides a link between the *text* and the *Context of Situation*. Genre affects the way that we interpret text. The categories of Narrative, Procedural, Hortatory, and Expository are generally used to describe genre.[18] A narrative has its own genre and it should not be analysed 'as if it were a scientific paper, a food recipe, or a piece of logical argumentation'.[19]

Third, the *Co-text* is 'the string of linguistic data within which a text is set'.[20] A reader predicts on the basis of the preceding *Co-text* what the next portion of text will most likely mean. Thus 'any sentence other than the first in a fragment of discourse, will have the whole of its interpretation forcibly constrained by the preceding text'.[21] Because the *Co-text* constrains the possible interpretations, it is possible to reconstruct some, or all, of the *extra-linguistic context* from the text and thus arrive at an interpretation (the more *Co-text*, the more secure the interpretation).[22]

A brief example will show the difference that *context* makes to a text. The sentence 'I am Esau your firstborn' is a text. It is grammatically complete and can be analysed in terms of its lexicogrammar. However, when its *context* is revealed by the preceding *Co-text*, 'Jacob said to his father' (Gen 27:19), the meaning changes significantly. Further reading of the *Co-text* would bring knowledge of the *Context of Situation* and this would reveal more of the significance of the sentence. Furthermore, knowledge of the *Context of Culture* would illuminate the significance of being the 'firstborn'.

---

15. Gillian Brown and George Yule, *Discourse Analysis* (Cambridge: Cambridge University Press, 2nd edition, 1983), 49-50.
16. Halliday and Hasan, *Language, context, and text*, 38.
17. Halliday and Hasan, *Language, context, and text*, 38-9.
18. Robert E Longacre, 'Discourse Peak as Zone of Turbulence', in *Beyond the Sentence: Discourse and Sentential Form*, edited by Jessica R Wirth (USA: Karoma Publishers, 1985), 83-98 at 83.
19. Robert E Longacre, *Holistic Textlinguistics*. http://www.sil.org/silewp/2003/silewp2003-004.pdf (SIL International, 2003), 3.
20. Green, 'Discourse Analysis', 183.
21. Brown and Yule, *Discourse Analysis*, 46, 234.
22. Peter Cotterell and Max Turner, *Linguistics and Biblical Interpretation* (London: SPCK. 1989), 17.

Functions of Text

Within the *Context of Culture* and *Context of Situation* an author will try to communicate his message to a recipient in a text.[23] In the Systemic-Functional Linguistics framework there are three functions of text: *Ideational*, *Interpersonal* and *Textual*. The *Ideational* function of language is what is usually understood as 'meaning'. It is what the text is about. The *Interpersonal* function concerns the social aspect of language and reveals the author's attitude to his or her environment and perceived relationship with his or her audience.[24] There are four possible *Interpersonal* functions of a clause: *Offers* (giving goods-and-services); *Commands* (demanding goods-and-services); *Statements* (giving information); and *Questions* (demanding information).[25] The author can also indicate the 'different graduations of probability from the speaker's point of view' through choice of verbal mood (indicative, subjunctive, optative) or through modal adjuncts.[26]

However, before analysing the *Ideational* and *Interpersonal* functions, the underlying relationships of constituents within the text; and between the text and context need to be established. These relationships are realised by the *Textual* function of language. The *Textual* function is 'not a way of using language, but rather a resource for ensuring that what is said is relevant and relates to its context'.[27] The two aspects of the *Textual* function are *Cohesion* (indications of continuity and discontinuity within a text) and *Prominence* (indications that certain ideas are more important than others).

Cohesion is created by the linguistic signals that an author will place in the text as clues to help the readers create an adequate 'mental representation' of the *Context of Situation*.[28] A high degree of *Cohesion* reduces the interpretive choices.[29] An author will also often divide a discourse into sections, and these sections may be divided into paragraphs. This is because a reader or hearer needs to process large amounts of information

---

23. Brown and Yule, *Discourse Analysis*, 24; Reed, *Philippians*, 25.
24. Reed, 'Discourse Analysis', 202-3.
25. Michael AK Halliday, and Christian MIM Matthiessen, *An Introduction to Functional Grammar* (London: Edwin Arnold, 3rd Edition, 2004), 107.
26. Reed, *Philippians*, 83.
27. Halliday and Hasan, *Language, context, and text*, 45.
28. Robert A Dooley and Stephen H Levinsohn, *Analysing Discourse: A Manual of Basic Concepts* (SIL International, 2000), 13.
29. Reed, *Philippians*, 88.

in 'chunks' which can be dealt with separately.[30] Although a paragraph is created by the presence of a single topic and a change of topic is the final indicator of a *Boundary*, there are grammatical features which provide evidence that supports the identification of these *Boundaries*.[31]

Prominence is the result of elements within the text that indicate that certain 'subjects, ideas or motifs of the author as more or less semantically and pragmatically significant than others'.[32] The term Prominence refers to a scale, a 'cline of prominence', rather than as an absolute description of importance.[33] There are typically three levels of *Prominence*: *Background*, *Mainline* and *Focus*. *Background* elements support the main argument by providing 'ancillary comments, explanations, conclusions and summaries'; *Mainline* elements are central to the author's purpose and carry the topics of the discourse; *Focal* elements are those which stand out.[34] It should be noted that *Prominence* is not intrinsic to the forms of language, but rather the way that these forms are used in a particular discourse. Thus in different discourses (and particularly in different genres) there will be different indicators of *Prominence*.[35]

Systemic Functional Linguistics categorises these indicators in terms of *Organic Ties* and *Componential Ties*.[36] *Componential Ties* 'concern the meaningful relationships between individual linguistic components'.[37] They are ties between components (words or phrases) which bind the discourse together. *Organic Ties* 'primarily concern the conjunctive systems of language'.[38] They are a way of describing the relationship between clauses, paragraphs and sections.[39] Shifts in these ties can also indicate *Boundaries* within the text. In Koine Greek there are also *morphosyntactic* features that serve as indicators. The features that are significant for *Cohesion* and *Prominence* in Colossians will be explained as they occur in the text.

---

30. Dooley and Levinsohn, *Analysing Discourse*, 18.
31. Levinsohn, *Discourse Features*, 271.
32. Reed, *Philippians*, 106.
33. Reed, *Philippians*, 108.
34. Reed, *Philippians*, 107.
35. Reed, *Philippians*, 111.
36. Halliday and Matthiessen, *Introduction to Functional Grammar*, 579.
37. Reed, *Philippians*, 93.
38. Reed, *Philippians*, 89.
39. Halliday and Matthiessen, *Introduction to Functional Grammar*, 536, 538.

The expository discourse of Colossians

The Genre and Cohesion of Colossians

Levinsohn notes that 'If the discourse features of the Greek text are taken into account when undertaking the exegesis of a passage, new interpretations of the passage should **not** normally be the result. Rather, […] it enables the exegete to choose between existing interpretations'.[40] The structure of Colossians is largely uncontroversial, so the results of a Discourse Analysis can be tested against generally accepted conclusions. It is generally agreed by commentators that the first section (1:1–2) and last section (4:7–18) are an epistolary prescript and conclusion which indicates that the discourse is an epistle.[41] Epistles typically contain expository and hortatory genres. In Colossians the mood of the verbs is predominately indicative (with occasional subjunctives) until 2:6 when imperatives start to appear, the dominance of which increases through the remainder of the epistle. Thus within the framework of an epistle, the discourse can be divided into two parts; an expository part (1:3 – 2:5) and a hortatory part (2:6 – 4:6). The following is an analysis of the *Cohesion* and *Prominence* of the first part of the letter.

The first two verses introduce the participants with references to Paul, Timothy, and those in Colossae. There is then repeated *Reference* to these Colossian recipients. *Reference* is a linguistic term for the use of pronouns or grammatical person and number of a verb to refer to linguistic items in the *Co-text*.[42] This creates
Componential Ties between these items. For example, *Componential Ties* are created in the discourse by the use of 2nd person plural pronouns (1:3, 4, 5, 6, 7, 8, 9, 12, 21, etc) and the repetition of 2nd person plural verb suffixes, such as ἔχετε (1:4), προηκούσατε (1:5) and ἐμάθετε (1:7). A more explicit *Componential Tie* is created by *Lexical Cohesion*. This refers to components that belong to the same *Semantic Domain*. A *Semantic Domain* is a group of words that have 'shared, distinctive, and supplementary semantic features'.[43] Relationships between words within a *Semantic*

---

40. Stephen H Levinsohn, 'The Relevance of Greek Discourse Studies to Exegesis' in the *Journal of Translation* 2/2 (2006): 20.
41. Peter T O'Brien, *Colossians, Philemon* (Waco: Word. 1982), 1, 246.
42. Reed, *Philippians*, 94.
43. Johannes P Louw and Eugene A Nida, (editors), *Greek-English Lexicon of the New Testament: based on semantic domains Volume 1: Introduction and Domains* (New York: UBS, 1988), vi.

Domain include *Repetition* and *Synonyms*. The simplest form of *Lexical Cohesion* is *Repetition* of lexical items. The repeated component does not have to be in the same form; both inflectional and derivational variations can create *Cohesion*.[44] However, *Repetition* of an item that is grammatically necessary (such as the article ὁ) does not indicate *Cohesion*.[45] *Synonyms* are lexical items from the same *Semantic Domain* that have closely related meanings.[46] A special case is *Antonyms* which refers to lexical items of opposite meaning.[47] *Repetition* of lexical items in the same *Semantic Domain* and *Reference* to them produces a pattern called a *semantic chain*. In Colossians, references to the author/s (often carried by 1st person verbs), references to 'Christ', and the adjective 'all' (πᾶς) produce *semantic chains* which give *Cohesion* to the whole epistle.

Section 1 (1:1-23)

The first major section of the epistle that has *Cohesion* is 1:1–23. This is indicated by three features. First, there is *Repetition* of Χριστός and Θεός with πατρός in reverse order (1:2, 3) thus forming a *chiasmus* which creates *Cohesion* between these verses.[48] *Chiasmus* is the commonly accepted label for 'inverted parallelism' (A B B' A'), where the interior elements (B B') are complementary and the exterior elements (A A') are complementary.[49] It should be noted that a *chiasmus* is identified on the basis of semantic content, rather than form.[50] However, it is likely that parallels between lexical components within the same *Semantic Domain* will reflect parallels in the semantic content. The second feature is an *inclusio*. This is formed by the recurrence of similar statements or lexical items at the beginning and end of a unit.[51] An *inclusio* is created between 1:4–7 and 1:23 by the *Repetition* of πίστις (1:4, 23), ἐλπίς (1:5, 23), εὐαγγέλιον (1:5, 23), ἀκούω (1:6, 23) and διάκονος (1:7, 23) in the same order. Third, the *semantic chain* formed by the *Repetition* of ἀκούω (1:4, 6, 9, 23) and the

---

44. Halliday and Matthiessen, Introduction to Functional Grammar, 571.
45. Reed, *Philippians*, 98.
46. Reed, *Philippians*, 98–9.
47. Halliday and Matthiessen, Introduction to Functional Grammar, 571.
48. Ernst R Wendland, 'Cohesion in Colossians: a structural-thematic outline', in *Notes on Translation* 6.3 (1992): 28–62 at 34.
49. Gregory T Christopher, 'A Discourse Analysis of Colossians 2:16 – 3:17', in *Grace Theological Journal* 11 (1990): 205–20 at 210.
50. Christopher, 'Colossians', 220.
51. George H Guthrie, *The Structure of Hebrews: A Text-Linguistic Analysis* (Leiden: Brill, 1994), 14.

Synonym προακούω (1:5) does not appear outside 1:3–23. These three features indicate both *Cohesion* of the text and mark the *Boundaries* of a distinct section which concludes at verse 23.[52]

Within this section, the present indicative verb, εὐχαριστοῦμεν, begins the *Mainline* of the exposition. There is then a *semantic chain* created by a strong concentration of *Reference* to the recipients (2nd person pronouns and verbs) in 1:3–8 followed by a large gap of 2nd person referents between verses 12 and 21. In verses 1:4–8 there is strong *Cohesion* between the clauses, with a mixture of *paratactic, hypotactic* and *embedded* clauses. There are also indications of a *Boundary* at verse 9. The phrase διὰ τοῦτο (1:9), which often indicates a resumption of the *Mainline* after intermediate supporting material, here refers back to the preceding paragraph.[53] The phrase ὑπὲρ ὑμῶν προσευχόμενοι (1:9) is a *back-reference* to 1:3. *Back-reference* is often used as a link to a preceding paragraph or point within a paragraph.[54] These two phrases indicate that 1:9 begins a new unit within the section and (noting the use of the present indicative παυόμεθα) gives strong reasons for concluding that this verse is a resumption of the *Mainline* after the intervening supporting material of 1:4–8. Verse 12 then concludes with εὐχαριστοῦντες τῷ πατρὶ, which forms an *inclusio* with εὐχαριστοῦμεν τῷ ... πατρί (1:3). These features indicate that 1:3–12 is a sub-section within 1:1–23 and that it comprises two paragraphs (1:4–8 and 1:9 12). The *Repetition* of the phrase 'bearing fruit and growing' (1:6, 10) and the *back-reference* of ἀφ' ἧς ἡμέρας (1:9; 1:6) give *Cohesion* between the paragraphs. The first paragraph (1:4–8) gives *Background* to the *Mainline* of thanksgiving. The next paragraph (1:9–12) is also *Background* as indicated by the subordinating conjunction ἵνα (along with the subjunctive πληρωθῆτε and dependant clauses). This *Background* indicates the desired result of the prayers. Therefore the *Mainline* of this sub-section is 'We give thanks for you when we pray'—*reason*—'we do not stop praying and asking'—*desired result*.

Verses 13 and 14 have continuity and discontinuity with both the preceding and following paragraphs, and thus form a *transition*. Verse 12 has described the Father as the one who has qualified the Colossians (ὑμᾶς)

---

52. Stephen H Levinsohn, *Discourse Features of New Testament Greek: A Coursebook on the Information Structure of New Testament Greek* (Dallas: Summer Institute of Linguistics, 2nd edition, 2000), 277–8.
53. Linda L Neeley, 'A Discourse Analysis of Hebrews', in *Occasional Papers in Translation and Textlinguistics* 3–4 (1987):1–146 at 18.
54. Neeley, 'Hebrews' 19; Guthrie, *Hebrews*, 99–100.

to share in the inheritance of the saints.⁵⁵ In verse 13, there is then a shift from 2ⁿᵈ to 1ˢᵗ person (the Father has rescued us (ἡμᾶς) from the power of darkness) which indicates a *Boundary*. However, across this *Boundary* there is *Cohesion* between the *Antonyms* φωτί (1:12) and σκότους (1:13). The relative clause (1:13) does not define the Father, and so is grammatically *dependant* on the preceding verse. This creates *Cohesion* and provides the *point of departure* for the following verses about the Son (1:14–20). The ties between verse 13 and 14 are strengthened by the continued *Reference* to 1st person in verse 14: 'in the Son we have redemption'. There is then a *semantic chain* of *Reference* to υἱός from verse 13 to 20. Within this is the widely recognised unit known as the 'Christ Hymn' (1:15–20).

The aspects of *parallelism, chiasmus*, lexical and semantic *Cohesion* in 1:15–20 have been widely described in commentaries and so will not be repeated here.⁵⁶ It is generally accepted as a *Cohesive* unit. This is also seen in the relationship between *Theme* and *Rheme* in each of the clauses. *Theme* is 'the element which serves as the point of departure of the message; it is that which locates and orients the clause within its context' and *Rheme* is the remainder of the message.⁵⁷ When the information in the *Rheme* of one clause becomes the *Theme* of the following clause, this gives *Cohesion* between the clauses.⁵⁸ For example, the *Rheme* of 'He is before all things' (1:17a) becomes the *Theme* of 'and all things in him hold together' (1:17b).

Parallel to the *Theme/Rheme* structure is the relationship of *Given Information* and *New Information*.⁵⁹ *Given Information* is that which is assumed to be known by the receptor.⁶⁰ For example, 1ˢᵗ person and 2ⁿᵈ person references are generally known in a epistle. *Given Information* is usually presented in the *Theme* and the *New Information* in the *Rheme*.⁶¹ When *New Information* is placed in the *Theme* rather than the *Rheme*, this indicates *Prominence*. Furthermore, as a result of various studies it appears that the unmarked word order in a Koiné Greek clause is for the

---

55. Note however the textual variant ἡμᾶς which (if accepted) would indicate an earlier shift to 1ˢᵗ person plural.
56. O'Brien, *Colossians*, 32-63; NT Wright, *The Epistles of Paul to the Colossians and to Philemon* (Grand Rapids: Eerdmans, 1986), 64–6.
57. Halliday and Matthiessen, *Introduction to Functional Grammar*, 64.
58. Longacre, *Holistic Textlinguistics*, 3.
59. Halliday and Matthiessen, *Introduction to Functional Grammar*, 88–9.
60. Halliday and Matthiessen, *Introduction to Functional Grammar*, 91.
61. Halliday and Matthiessen, *Introduction to Functional Grammar*, 93.

verb to precede the object.[62] A constituent that precedes the verb and is associated with *Given Information* has *Mainline Prominence*. A constituent that precedes the verb and is associated with *New Information* has *Focal Prominence*. Therefore the 'Son' has *Mainline Prominence* throughout this unit, as indicated by the marked word order: ἐν αὐτῷ, αὐτός and δι' αὐτοῦ preceding the verb in each clause (1:16, 17, 18, 19, 20).

There is also a strong connection between this unit and the rest of the epistle. There is *Lexical Cohesion* created by *Repetition* of οὐρανός (1:5, 16, 20, 23) and γῆ (1:16, 20), with possible *Collocation* of κόσμος and κτίσις (1:6, 23) as *Antonyms* of οὐρανός. *Collocation* refers to *Lexical Cohesion* between components that is derived from the *Co-text* or *Context of Situation* rather than their *Semantic Domain*.[63] The more frequently that two items are *Collocated* in the same *genre* the stronger the *Cohesion* between them. These *Componential Ties* form a *semantic chain* that binds this unit to the surrounding section. In addition, the unit is tied to the preceding one by the lexical *Repetition* of ἐξουσία (1:13, 16) and the *Synonymous* relationship of βασιλεία (1:13) and θρόνοι (1:16). The unit is tied to the following one by the lexical *Repetition* of ἀποκαταλλάσσω (1:20, 23), the *Collocation* of σταυρός (1:20) and θάνατος (1:22) (which are related to the concept of death), and the *Antonyms* εἰρηνοποιήσας (1:20) and ἐχθροί (1:21). The first occurrence of σῶμα (1:18) also starts a *semantic chain* that continues until the end of chapter 2. There is also a possible link between 'all the fullness' dwelling (κατοικῆσαι) in him (1:19) and the conditional remaining (ἐπιμένετε) in faith (1:23), because these share the same *Semantic Domain*.[64] Furthermore, many of the words and phrases of this unit are repeated in 2:9-12. The phrases ἐν αὐτῷ (2:9), ὅς ἐστίν (2:10), and ἐν ᾧ (2:11) echo the style of the hymn. 'God was pleased to have all his fullness dwell in him' (1:19) is restated as 'in him all the fullness of the Deity lives in bodily form' (2:9). Also, ἡ κεφαλή is repeated (1:18; 2:10) and the phrase πάσης ἀρχῆς καὶ ἐξουσίας (2:10, 15) is a *back-reference* to 1:13, 16, and 18. However, in this later unit, the content of the 'hymn' is expanded. Thus it appears likely that the unit was written as part of the epistle or that the epistle was written around the unit.

---

62. Reed *Philippians*, 116; Levinsohn, 'Relevance', 11; Stanley E Porter, *Idioms of the Greek New Testament* (Sheffield: Sheffield Academic Press, 1994), 293.
63. Halliday and Matthiessen, *Introduction to Functional Grammar*, 571.
64. Louw and Nida, *Greek-English Lexicon*, 724.

The καὶ ὑμᾶς of verse 21 is usually seen as a mark of a new beginning.[65] However, according to Levinsohn, καί usually 'constrains the material it introduces to be processed as being added to and associated with previous material [...] it does *not* represent a new development'.[66] So, can this clause be interpreted as an addition to a previous idea or is this the exception that proves the rule? There are three indications that it is an addition to the previous paragraph. First, the object of the main clause (νυνὶ δὲ ἀποκατήλλαξεν) is ὑμᾶς. The previous 2nd person plural was in 1:12. Thus, after a lengthy digression to 1st person (1:13–14) and 3rd person references (1:15–20), the καὶ ὑμᾶς re-establishes the address to the recipients. Second, although it is not immediately obvious, the lexical *Repetition* of ἀποκαταλλάσσω (1:20, 23) indicates that the clause is semantically an *extension* of the reconciliation of all things, which is grammatically dependant on 1:19. Thus its subject is likely to be πᾶν τὸ πλήρωμα (1:19), which is most likely a reference to God.[67] Third, following the *Mainline* of this sub-section, Paul has stated that the Father has rescued 'us' from darkness (1:13a) and the Father has brought 'us' into the kingdom of his Son (1:13b) and Paul has described who the Son is (1:15–20). Given that background, he now says that God (τὸ πλήρωμα) has reconciled the Colossians (1:21–22).[68] Thus there is a strong connection with the preceding material in the section in terms of subject, object and topic, which explains the use of καί.

The Colossians have not been previously identified as alienated or enemies. Therefore, this is *New Information* and they have *Focal Prominence*. The νυνί has temporal force (contrasting with ποτε) and δέ indicates that the phrase is a new development which progresses the argument (1:21).[69] The shift from aorist indicative to present indicative ἐπιμένετε (1:23) and the particle γε indicates that this clause has greater *Prominence* relative to the surrounding verses.[70] The following clauses have unmarked word order and are *Background*. However, the use of a redundant pronoun (if it were omitted there would be no ambiguity) and full noun phrase with a 1st person singular verb in the clause 'of which I Paul have become a servant' (1:23) shifts *Focus* to Paul as an individual (rather than Paul and Timothy)

---

65. O'Brien, *Colossians*, 64.
66. Levinsohn, *Discourse Features*, 124.
67. O'Brien, *Colossians*, 51–3.
68. Wendland, 'Colossians', 39
69. Levinsohn, 'Relevance', 18.
70. Reed, *Philippians*, 119.

and also contrasts with the recipients in the previous clauses.[71] This also provides further evidence of the existence of a *Boundary* at this point.

Therefore the section (1:1–23) appears to be comprised of two sub-sections, within which are a number of distinct paragraphs. The first sub-section (1:3–12) begins the *Mainline* of the epistle and contains two paragraphs (1:4–8 and 1:9–12). The second sub-section (1:13–23) contains a transition from the previous sub-section (1:13–14), a paragraph (1:15–20) and a continuation of the *Mainline* (1:21–23). Analysis of features in the text has shown the *Cohesion* of this section as well as identifying its *Mainline* and *Focus*. The *Mainline* is initially presented as a prayer (1:3, 9) which draws on the *Background* information that the Colossians already knew (1:4–8). Further *Background* information is presented regarding the goal of their life (1:9–12) and the nature of Christ (1:15–20), which supports the *Mainline* of the reality of their rescue and reconciliation (1:13–14, 21–22). The *Mainline* reaches a climax with the requirement that they remain in Christ (1:23).

Section 2 (1:24–2:5)

The *semantic chain* of 1st person references to Paul is the most striking element of the next section and gives clear *Cohesion* to it. The preceding reference to the Paul (1:23) acts as a *Hooked Key Word* (a component which creates a transition by referring forward to a subsequent paragraph) that links to the *semantic chain* of 1st person singular references in this section.[72] There is also a *semantic chain* of μυστήριον (1:26, 1:27, 2:2) along with other words in the same *Semantic Domain* (making known / keeping secret); the *Synonyms* ἀποκεκρυμμένον (1:26) and ἀπόκρυφοι (2:3), and their *Antonyms* ἐφανερώθη (1:26), γνωρίσαι (1:27), εἰδέναι (2:1), ἐπί γνῶσιν (2:2), and γνώσεως (2:3) which give further *Cohesion*. The semantic chain of σῶμα (1:18, 22, 24; 2:11, 17, 19, 23; 3:15) creates *Cohesion* with the previous and following sections, while the use of words related to life and death (2:12 – 3:7) give cohesion with the following section.

While the *Cohesion* of 1:24–2:5 is clear, the exact relationship between paragraphs within the section is not. Wendland proposes that 1:24–29 forms a *chiasmus*.[73] However, although the conjunctions and relative pronouns tie these verses together, *Componential Ties* are not apparent in

---

71. Reed, *Philippians*, 116.
72. Guthrie, *Hebrews*, 100.
73. Wendland, 'Colossians', 40.

these six verses and so a *chiasmus* is unlikely. However, there does seem to be a lexical *chiasmus* through the whole section with forms of χαίρω (1:24; 2:5), σάρξ (1:24; 2:5) ἀποκρύπτω / ἀπόκρυφος (1:26; 2:3), and πλοῦτος with μυστήριον (1:27; 2:2). This suggests that 1:24-27 and 2:2–5 may be paragraphs which bracket two central units (1:28 and 1:29 – 2:1).

In the first unit (1:24–27) the indicative present verb χαίρω commences the *Mainline* as indicated by νῦν.[74] The second clause continues the *Mainline*, as indicated by καί and the present indicative ἀνταναπληρῶ. Thus the topic of the *Mainline* of this unit is found in the phrases 'I rejoice in the sufferings' (1:24a) and 'I fulfil the afflictions in my flesh' (1:24b). The *Background* to this is then given in dependant relative clauses: 'I have become a servant of the church' (1:25), and the purpose: 'to fulfil the λόγος of God' (1:25), the content of which is 'the mystery that has been hidden' (1:26a) but now 'revealed (ἐφανερώθη) to the saints' (1:26b), to whom 'God wished (ἠθέλησεν) to make known the riches of the mystery' (1:27). However, Paul remains in *Focus* as indicated by ἐγώ (1:25).

In the second unit (1:28) the present indicative καταγγέλλομεν resumes the *Mainline*. However, the 1st person plurals of this verse contrast with the singulars of the surrounding verses and give it added *Prominence*. As there is a change of reference from singular to plural, the pronoun ἡμεῖς is not for emphasis but for clarity. However, the three-fold *Repetition* of πάντα ἄνθρωπον does give *Focal Prominence*. The ἵνα with subjunctive gives the *Background* to this proclamation.

Wendland identifies a *chiasmus* of ἀγωνιζόμενος . . . ἐνέργειαν . . . ἐνεργουμένην . . . ἀγῶνα that gives *Cohesion* to the third unit (1:29 – 2:1).[75] The *Mainline* of the exposition continues with the present indicative κοπιῶ (1:29). The nature of this labour is described with two dependant participial phrases. The assertion that Paul is labouring is strengthened by the following clause (2:1) as indicated by γάρ.[76] Furthermore, the use of θέλω and the perfect infinitive εἰδέναι addresses the recipients directly and gives *Focal Prominence* to the statement ἡλίκον ἀγῶνα ἔχω ὑπὲρ ὑμῶν κτλ.

In the fourth unit (2:2–5) Paul draws on the exposition of 1:24–27 in inverted order to give the purpose of the labouring and agonising. Now 'the riches of the knowledge of the mystery' (2:2) are 'hidden

---

74. Reed, *Philippians*, 119.
75. Wendland, 'Colossians', 41.
76. Levinsohn, 'Relevance', 18.

(ἀπόκρυφοι) in Christ' (2:3) rather than 'hidden (ἀποκρύπτω) from ages and generations' (1:26). The exposition is returned to the *Mainline* by the present indicative λέγω (2:4) and, since words of 'saying' often signal 'upcoming, thematic material', this phrase gives *Prominence* to what follows.[77] The ἵνα introduces a subordinate *Background* clause, however the phrase μηδεὶς ὑμᾶς (2:4) retains *Focal Prominence*. This is firstly because the clause has marked word order (subject and object precede verb) and secondly because the *Reference* μηδείς is the first mention of someone whom the Colossians need to be warned about and so it provides *New Information*. Placing this *New Information* in the *Theme* of the clause (rather than the *Rheme*) gives *Focal Prominence*. The implied warning is about πιθανολογίᾳ (2:4) which contrasts with the λόγος of God (1:25). This anticipates the *Mainline* of the next section and explains Paul's purpose in writing. This is strengthened (γάρ) by the final verse; although Paul is 'absent in the flesh', he is 'rejoicing in their steadfastness' (2:5).

Therefore, an analysis of *Cohesion* and *Prominence* in the first part of the epistle identified that the first section (1:3–23) draws primarily on *Given Information* (what the Colossians have heard), introduces the topic of remaining in Christ (1:23) and establishes the background of what the Colossians had heard. The final clause introduces *New Information*; Paul as a servant of the gospel. This provides the topic for the second section (1:24 – 2:5), which is an expository section that provides predominately *New Information* for the Colossians about Paul and his proclamation about Christ. The topic of this section is centred on Paul's actions.

The content of his actions is given *Focal Prominence* in the two central units; 'proclaiming Christ' and 'wanting them to know his agony'. Paul focuses on proclaiming that the location of the riches is in Christ so that the Colossians will not be deceived (2:4). Typically the focus on Paul in this section is explained simply by the fact that Paul has not previously met the Colossians (2:1).[78] However, the *Focal Prominence* of 2:4 indicates that this section is a necessary contribution to Paul's argument in the rest of the epistle (2:6 – 4:6) which is a hortatory presentation of his main argument, based on the background of the first two sections. The above description of *Cohesion* and *Prominence* of Colossians 1:1 – 2:5 lays the foundation upon which the significance of the *Ideational* and *Interpersonal* aspects

---

77. Reed, *Philippians*, 112.
78. Wright, *Colossians*, 86.

could be investigated. The relationship between the text and the *Context of Situation* could then also be analysed.

Conclusions

Discourse Analysis takes analysis beyond the sentence and questions what the larger units are and how they relate. It is useful for identifying appropriate divisions within a discourse, determining the main topics of a discourse and identifying possible misinterpretations of the *Prominence* of these topics. A Systemic-Functional approach to the analysis of the features of *Cohesion* and *Prominence* does not provide tools for reaching a consensus (there can be differing interpretations amongst those who practice Discourse Analysis). However it does provide a method for analysing discourse and a meta-language for describing one's analysis and evaluating competing interpretations. A broader benefit of a Systemic-Functional Linguistics approach is that it enables one to analyse one aspect of this framework without the illusion that it is a complete analysis. Furthermore, even if a thorough analysis is not performed, being aware of these features increases one's sensitivity to the text and improves one's exegesis.

List of Contributors

Elizabeth Boase is Lecturer in Old Testament at the Uniting College, Adelaide and in the School of Theology at Flinders University.

Alan H Cadwallader is Senior Lecturer in Biblical Studies at the Australian Catholic University.

Anne Elvey is President of the Fellowship of Biblical Studies and an adjunct research fellow in the Centre for Comparative Literature and Cultural Studies at Monash University and an Honorary Research Associate at Melbourne College of Divinity.

Terence E Fretheim is the Elva B Lovell Professor of Old Testament at Luther Seminary, Minnesota.

Shelly Li is Assistant Manager of the Post Graduate Research Programme at the Lee Kong Chian School of Business, Singapore Management University.

William Loader is Emeritus Professor at Murdoch University and an Australian Research Council Professorial Fellow.

Philip McKeown is a postgraduate of Moore Theological College, Sydney.

Ockert S Meyer followed an academic and pastoral ministry in South Africa before migrating to Australia. He has recently retired from Yarralumla Uniting Church in Canberra.

Chris Mulherin is an Anglican priest and doctoral student with the Australian College of Theology.

Frank S Ravitch is Professor of Law at the Michigan State University College of Law.

Index of Biblical References and Ancient Texts

Genesis		Leviticus	
1	68	11	82
1:26–28	8	17 – 18	87
3:16–17	37		
6:5 – 9:17	34	Deuteronomy	
6:5–7	37	8:2	36
6:5	35, 37, 38	9:4–5	46
6:6–7	35	10:16	90
6:6	37	14:7	111
6:7	36	26:5–9	33
6:11–13	35	30:6	90
6:19	35		
7:6	35	Psalms	57, 60
7:10–12	35	7:12–16	40
7:15–16	35	22:1	54
7:17–20	35	40:6	88
7:24	35	51:16–17	88
8:17	35	77:4–10	33
8:20–21	39	78:40–41	37
8:21	38	84:10	119
9:5	35		
9:8–17	39	Proverbs	
12:1–3	134	22:8	41
15:5–6	134		
17:10–14	93	Ecclesiastes	
18–19	39	9:11	41
18:25	41		
22:12	36	Isaiah	
27:19	142	10:12–19	43
		29:13	80
Exodus		47:1–15	43
3:14	68	49:14	54
20:5b	42	54:7–8	54
22:21–24	43	59:17–18	40
32:7–14	45	63:7–10	37
34:6–7	33, 62	64:5–9	40
34:7	42	64:6–7	35

Index

Jeremiah	
3:7	43
3:19–20	43
4:4	90
5:9	42
6:11	40
6:19	40, 41
7:18–20	40
12:1	41
13:14	42
14:10	42
14:16	41
17:10	41
19:7–9	35
21:7	42
21:12–14	40
21:14	42
25:12–14	42
25:14	43
27:6–7	42
38:17–18	44
42:10	43
44:7–8	40
46:21	42
50–51	42
50:24–25	40
50:29	41, 43
51:24	43

Lamentations	49ff
1	55, 57
1:1	55
1:1–9b	50
1;2	55
1:5	57, 59
1:6	55
1:8	57, 59
1:9	55, 59
1:9c	50
1:10–11b	50
1:11	55
1:11c–16	50
1:12	54, 55
1:13	54
1:14	54, 57, 59
1:16	55
1:17	50, 55
1:18	54, 55, 57, 59
1:18–19	55
1:18–22	50
1:19	55
1:20	55, 59
1:21	54, 55
1:22	57
2	55
2:1–9	52
2:1–20	50
2:1	52
2:2	52
2:3–5	52–3
2:3	52
2:4	52
2:5	52
2:6–8	53
2:6	52, 53
2:7	52
2:8	53
2:9	52
2:11–13	51
2:14	59
2:18–19	55
2:18	55
2:20–22	50
3	56, 57, 60, 63
3:1–18	53
3:1–41	50
3:5	53
3:7	53
3:11	53
3:12	53
3:13	53
3:17–18	53
3:20–32	62
3:21	57
3:21–39	57
3:22–23	57
3:22–24	57, 63
3:25–30	57–8
3:31–33	57, 58
3:34–39	57, 58
3:39	59
3:40–41	55
3:41–42	58
3:42	56, 59
3:42–47	50
3:43–44	56

3:48–66	50	15:27	116, 117
3:55–66	56	16:5–12	85
3:64–66	40	17:1–9	7
4:1–16	50	22:38–40	33
4:6	59	23:2–4	86
4:13	59	23:23	85
4:17–20	50		
4:21–22	50	Mark	80f
5	56	1:22	86
5:1	56	2:9	81, 89
5:1–22	50	2:10	81
5:7	59	2:14–15	83
5:16	59	2:17a	81
5:20	54, 56	2:17b	81
5:21–22	56	2:25–27	81
5:22	56	2:27	89, 92
		2:28	81
Ezekiel		3:4	89
7:27	41	4:10	81
17:22–24	92	4:30–32	92
22:31	40	5	83
		6 – 8	82
Hosea		7	86
4:1–3	35, 41	7:1–23	80
6:6	86	7:2–4	85
		7:3–4	80
Jonah		7.5	80
4:2	33	7:6–8	80
		7:9–13	80
Zechariah		7:14–15	81
1:15	42, 43	7:15	92, 94
		7:17	81
Matthew	84f	7:18a	81
5:17–19	84	7:18b – 19	81
5:17–20	84	7:18b	85
5:21–48	84, 86	7:19b	81
7:6	99	7:20–23	81
7:29	86	7:24–30	83, 97, 99
9:13	86	7:24	106
11:28–30	86	7:26	106
12:7	86	7:27	110
13:31–32	92	7:28	116, 117
13:52	86	8:14–21	82
15:1–20	84f	8:17–21	81
15:11	85	8:22–26	83
15:20	85	9:2–10	7
15:21–28	99	9:28	81
15:24	100	9:37	88

10:2–9	87	6:1	94
10:2–12	88	7:1–6	94
10:9	89	8:1–4	94
10:10	81	11:25–26	94
10:17–22	92	13:8–10	94
12:17	89		
12:27	89	1 Corinthians	125f
12:29–30	90	1:10	127
13:11	88	5:1	128
		6:15–20	128
Luke	86f	11:18	127
7:1–10	88	12	129
9:28–36	7	12:25	127
9:31	7	13	132
11:42	85	13:4	132
13:18–19	92	14	125, 136
16:16	86	14:5	135
16:17	87	14:33	127
16:18	87	14:34	125, 135
		14:34–35	135, 136, 137
John		14:40	127
1:17	94	15:3–4	33
6:6	109		
6:63	94	Galatians	
18:16	119	1:6–9	93
		1:9	93
Acts		2:1–10	93
3:1	87	2:11–14	82, 93
5:12	87	3:1–5	93
5:25	87	3:15–22	94
6:13	87	3:28	32, 111
6:14	91	5:13–15	94
10	108	5:22–23	94
10:9–16	87	6:7	41
10:17	87		
10:28	87	Ephesians	100, 137
10:34	88	2:14–15	83
15	93		
20:20–22	86	Philippians	
21:21	91	3:2–4	93
26:3	91	3:2	110
28:17	91	3:18–19	93
Romans	94	Colossians	92, 137, 139f
2:25–29	94	1:1–23	146f, 151
3:1–8	94	1:1 – 2:5	153
3:31	94	1:1–2	145
4:1–22	94	1:2	141, 146

1:3	145, 146, 147, 151	1:26b	152
1:3–8	147	1:27	151, 152
1:3–12	151	1:28	152
1:3–23	147, 153	1:29 – 2:1	152
1:3–2:5	145	1:29	152
1:4–7	146	2:1	151, 152
1:4–8	141, 147, 151	2:2–5	152
1:4	145, 146	2:2	151, 152
1:5	145, 146, 147, 149	2:3	151, 152, 153
1:6	145, 146, 147, 149	2:4	153
1:7	145	2:5	152, 153
1:7–8	141	2:6–4:6	145
1:8	145	2:6	145
1:9	145, 146, 147, 151	2:9–12	149
1:9–12	147, 151	2:9	149
1:10	147	2:10	149
1:12	145, 147, 148, 150	2:11	149, 151
1:13	147, 148, 149	2:12 – 3:7	151
1:13a	150	2:15	149
1:13b	150	2:17	151
1:13–14	150, 151	2:19	151
1:13–20	148	2:23	151
1:13–23	151	3:15	151
1:14–20	148	4:7–18	145
1:14	147, 148	4:9	141
1:15–20	148, 150, 151		
1:16	149	Hebrews	94 5
1:17	149	7:18	94
1:17a	148	9:13–14	94
1:17b	148		
1:18	149, 151	2 Peter	
1:19	149, 150	2:22	99
1:20	149		
1:21	145, 147, 149, 150	**Other Ancient Texts**	
1:21–22	150, 151		
1:21–23	151	1 Clement	125f
1:22	151	1.1	126, 133
1:23	146, 147, 149, 150–1, 153	2.2	126
		2.6	126
1:24	152	3.2	126
1:24a	152	3.3	133
1:24b	152	3.4	126
1:24–27	152	4.12	126
1:24–29	151	9.4	127
1:24 – 2:5	151, 153	10 – 12	134
1:25	152, 153	10	133
1:26	151, 152	11	133
1:26a	152	11.2	127, 133

12	133
12.1	133
12.7	134
12.8	133
14:2	126
15.1	126
16.5	126
19.2	126
20.1	126
20.3	127
20.9	126
20.10	127
21.1	127, 131
22.5	127
24.1	135
30.3	127
34.7	127
34.8	135
37.2–3	131
37:5 – 38:2	128, 135
41.1	135
43.2	126
44.3–6	127
44.6	133
46.7	126
46.9	126
47	127, 135
47.1–3	128
47.6	126, 133
47.7	133
48.1	128
49	132
49.5	127, 132
49:5–6	135
50.4	131
50.5	127, 132
51.1	126
51.2	131
51.3	126
54.2	126
54.4	131
55.1	126
56.12	126
57.1	126
60.3	127
60.4 – 61.3	126
60.4	127
61.1	127
62.2	127
63.1	126
63.2	126, 127
63.3	133
63.4	126
64.1	127
65.1	127, 133

1 Enoch
1 – 5	90

1 QM/1Q33
7.6–7	81

11 QT^a/11Q19
46.13–16	81

Bede
2.7	107

Catena in Acta (Catena Andreae)
176.6	105

Letter of Aristeas
234	88

Tertullian
On Prayer
6.3	110

Index to Modern Authors

Abram, D	1, 15	Bonhoeffer, D	65, 75-7, 78
Albrektson, B	55	Boomershine, TE	116
Alford, H	106	Booth, RP	88, 89
Allison, DC	84, 88, 89, 116	Boring, ME	82
Alter, R	51	Bowe, BE	131
Arnold, M	109	Braaten, CE	101
Balentine, S	55	Brenner, A	4
Bandinei, J	99, 103	Briggs, S	97
Banks, R	81, 84	Brown, G	142, 143
Bar-Efrat, S	51	Brown, R	136
Barnes, A	99	Bruce, AB	99, 105, 110
Barrett, CK	86	Brueggeman, W	43, 54, 61
Bartkowski, J	14	Cadwallader, AH	97ff, 104
Bass, JH	103	Cahill, T	74
Bauer, DR	84	Calabresi, SG	14
Baur, FC	101	Campbell, DA	79
Beal, TK	61	Carson, DA	140
Becker, J	88	Carter, W	85
Bengel, JA	99, 103, 107	Chadwick, GA	99, 105, 106, 111
Bengel ME	99, 103, 107	Chadwick, O	111
Benson, A	100, 106	Charlesworth, JH	80
Benson, EW	116	Christopher, GT	146
Bergant, D	61	Chryssavgis, J	6-8
Berges, U	59, 63	Colenso, JW	110, 111
Berkhof, H	66	Coleridge, M	123
Blass, F	103	Collins, AY	86
Blomberg, CL	86	Collins, JJ	91
Bloomfield, ST	103, 107, 110	Collins, R	136
Blondell, E	105	Conzelmann, H	86, 136
Blount, BK	122	Cotterell, P	142
Blunt, JH	99	Counet, PC	59
Boase, EC	49ff	Cowan, H	99, 106, 115
Bobbit, P	17	Craik, GM	114
Bobrick, B	12	Crossley, JG	80
Bock, D	86	Crouch, JE	104
Boecker, HJ	57	Cunnington, CW	116

Dale, RW	98, 100, 106	Grimes, JE	141
Davies, WD	88, 89, 116	Grimké, SM	117, 123
Deines, R	84	Grondin, J	15, 17
Demers, P	102	Griesbach, JJ	106
Dibelius, M	136	Gruen, ES	91
Dobbs-Allsopp, FW	51, 52, 53, 61, 63	Guthrie, GH	146, 147, 151
Docker, J	2	Gwatkin, HM	100
Donahue, JR	89	Habel, NC	4
Donaldson, JW	102	Haggis, J	2
Dooley, RA	143, 144	Halliday, MAK	140-6, 148, 149
Dowling, EV	4	Hallowell, AD	101, 113
Dunn, JDG	79, 85, 88, 89, 90, 92, 93	Harrington, DJ	89, 92
		Harrisville, RA	97
Eaton, H	4	Hassan, R	140, 141
Edersheim, A	99, 100, 120	Hasting, J	99
Eliade, M	91	Hermann, W	114
Ellicott, CJ	98, 99	Heschel, AJ	65, 67-75, 77, 78
Elvey, AF	1ff, 7	Hessel, DT	6
Eskridge, WN	15, 16	Hill, B	120
Exell, JS	105, 110	Hillers DR	55
Farrar, FW	98, 105, 106, 110	Hollingdale, RJ	23
Firth, F	130	Holmén, T	88, 92
Fischer, G	2	Hope, JW	106
Fitzmyer, JA	87	Hopkins, E	123
Ford, J	119	Horrell, D	125, 126, 132
Foster, P	84	Horsley, RA	81
France, RT	81, 82, 84, 85	Horsley, S	107, 119
Freed, M	109	Hort, FJA	109, 116, 117
Fretheim TE	29ff, 37, 42, 43, 50, 54, 58-62	Hübner, H	87
		Innis, R	22
Freyne, S	80	Jackson-McCabe, M	85
Fritzsche, CF	110	Jeffers, JS	126, 130, 131
Froehlich, K	29, 50	Jervell, J	86, 87
Froude, JA	101	Johnson, LT	136
Gadamer, H-G	12, 13, 15-17, 22	Jowett, B	109, 115
Gadesden, F	102, 114, 118	Kachur, RM	120
Gaiser, FJ	40	Kähler, M	101, 109, 122
Garvie, AE	99, 104	Kartsonis, A	7
Gatta, J	7	Käsemann, E	88
Geertz, C	16	Kaye, B	101
Gerstenberger, E	51	Kazen, T	85, 88
Gilman, CP	112	Keller, C	7
Glatzer, NN	67	Kermode, F	52
Gordis, R	56	Klein, H	87
Gottlieb, H	53, 55	Klinghardt, M	87
Gould, E	104, 106, 107, 111, 115	Kolitz, S	72
		Krasovec, J	57
Green, D	113	Kraus, HJ	57
Green, JB	139, 141, 142	Kristeva, J	8
Grey, TC	11, 13, 18	Kuske, M	76

Kwok, P-l	1	Mott, L	101, 113, 114, 123
Lake, K	126	Mulherin, C	21ff
Lambert, JC	99	Müller, K	85
Lanahan, WF	50	Munro, W	130, 136
Landy, F	52	Murray, JOF	117
Lawrence, FG	15	Neeley, LL	147
Lee, DA	5-6	Nida, EA	145, 149
Lesnick, H	11	Nietzsche, F	23, 24
Levinas, E	68, 73-5	Nolland, JH	84, 85, 89
Levinson, S	11	O'Brien, PT	145, 148, 150
Levinsohn, SH	139, 143-5, 147-50	O'Connor, KM	51, 53
Li, S	125ff	O'Neill, JC	99
Liddell, HG	103	Olshausen, H	99, 100, 112, 114, 119
Lightfoot, JB	101, 107, 109-10, 113	Penchansky, D	54
Linafelt, T	56, 61	Penelope, J	102
Lindsay, M	111, 115, 120, 121	Perry, MJ	11
Loader, W	79ff, 82, 83, 85, 87, 92, 94	Plöger, O	57
		Plummer, A	104
Longacare, RE	142, 148	Plumptre, EH	98, 99, 106, 107, 111
Louw, JP	139, 145, 149	Plumwood, V	3
Luckock, HM	105, 106, 119	Polanyi, M	21-6
Luz, U	82, 85, 89, 104	Pomeroy, SB	112
Lynch, TT	113	Poorthuis, MJHM	88
M'Farlane, J	110, 112	Porter, SE	139, 140, 149
MacDonald, MY	133	Powell, HJ	14
MacEvilly, Bp	104, 118	Powell, MA	84
Maclaren, A	100	Prickett, S	101, 109
Malina, BJ	81	Prosch, H	26
Marcus, J	82, 86, 89, 92	Provan, I	55
Maritz, P	94	Rabinovitz, NS	103
Matthiessen, CMIM	143, 144, 146, 148, 149	Räisänen, H	89
		Ravitch, FS	11ff, 12, 13, 14, 17, 18, 19
Maurice, FD	114		
McKane, W	43	Redditt, PL	54
McKinlay, JE	2	Reed, JL	80
McKeown, P	139ff	Reed, JT	139-41, 144 -6, 149-53
Meier, JP	84	Reid, BE	3
Melnyk, J	109	Renan, E	98, 101, 108, 111
Metzger, BM	116	Rich, A	8
Meyer, OS	65ff	Richlin, A	103
Michie, H	98, 117, 118	Roberts, RD	102
Mill, J	106	Robbins, B	120
Milne, P	4	Robinson, JA	100
Mintz, A	57, 60, 85	Rosenzweig, F	67
Miskotte, KH	65, 67, 68, 69, 73, 74	Ruether, RR	1,3,6
Mohrlang, R	84	Rummel, E	118
Moloney, FJ	82	Russell, B	114
Moreton-Robinson, A	2	Russell, LM	1, 2
Morison, J	100, 104, 106, 107, 117, 118	Russell, P	114
		Safran, L	7

Salo, K	87	Veijola, T	88
Samuelson, NM	74	van Belle, G	94
Sanders, EP	79, 88, 89	van der Watt, JG	94
Sanders, J	43	von Harnack, A	66, 114
Sariola, H	80	von Rad, G	42
Sayers, J	114	Wace, H	100
Schech, S	2	Waetjen, C	116
Schleusner, JF	103	Wainwright, E	2, 8, 9
Schmidt, C	111	Ward, M	109, 124
Schneiders, SM	5	Watson, F	viii, 79, 93
Schodde, GH	108	Weinsheimer, J	12
Scholz, JMA	106	Weiss, B	106, 108, 110, 115
Schütz, J	127	Wells, J	114
Schüssler Fiorenza, E	1-5, 8, 102, 120	Wendland, ER	146
Schwartz, H	70, 71	Westcott BF	101, 102, 103, 109, 116
Schwartz, J	88	Westermann, C	55, 57, 61
Schwarzschild, M	11	West, C	4
Scott, R	103	Westerholm, SG	79
Scrivener, FH	106	Weymouth, R	116
Seeley, JR	110, 111, 119	White, EG	106, 111
Segovia, FF	2	Wilke, SG	103
Selbie, JA	99	Williams, I	98, 101, 113, 119
Selvidge, MJ	102, 103	Wilson, SG	88, 91
Sigal, P	79, 85	Wind, R	77
Silva, M	140	Wire, A	135
Sittser, GL	6	Wirth, JR	142
Smith, D	98, 103, 104	Witherington, B	82
Snodgrass, KR	84, 85	Wollstonecraft, M	123
Stanton, EC	2, 121	Wood, JG	104
Stapfer, E	106	Wright, NT	78, 148
Stendel, JCF	99	Wright, WA	98
Stock, A	98	Yellin, JF	2
Strange, LS	2	Yule, G	142, 143
Sugirtharajah, RS	112	Zenger, E	46
Sun, H	40		
Swete, HB	104, 106, 107, 110, 111		
Syreni, K	88		
Tennyson, A	115, 116		
Thackeray, HStJ	103		
Thayer, JH	127		
Theissen, G	127		
Thorpe, M	111		
Tischendorf, C	106		
Tomson, PJ	88		
Trainor, M	104		
Tregelles, SP	106		
Trible, P	1		
Tucker, G	40		
Turner, M	142		

Milton Keynes UK
Ingram Content Group UK Ltd.
UKHW021823020823
426224UK00013B/676